MONEY, POWER AND SEX

The Lori Vallow Daybell Trial By Juror Number 18

Tom Evans

Milwuakee Wisconsin USA

Published by:
Genius Book Publishing
PO Box 250380
Milwaukee Wisconsin 53225 USA
GeniusBookPublishing.com

ISBN: 978-1-958727-31-7

240519 Digest LH

Table of Contents

In memory of Emily and Sarah. Not long after the trial ended domestic violence hit way too close to home

INTRODUCTION

This is my first attempt at writing a book. I have always wanted to do so, but it's a big-time commitment and a lot of work, so I guess I needed the proper motivation. I sure wasn't looking for it in this way and I had no thoughts of writing a book when I found myself on the jury for the Lori Vallow Daybell trial. I can't really explain why I decided to write this book. I don't really understand it myself, but it's just something I felt I had to do by the time the trial was over. I will say that by the time the trial was over I knew two things: first, I was struggling to find a way to gain some good out of my experience, and second, I felt the need to tell the story of all the good I saw. The good did not erase the horror I was exposed to, but it did offset it some.

This was also my first time serving on a jury and I always thought that, when called upon, you served your time and then went back to normal life when the trial ended. That was my intention going into this trial. I was anxious about the time I would have to spend away from what I had planned and hoping it would be over quickly so I could get back to it. For a lot of reasons, it didn't work out that way for me. It just wasn't as simple as that. When the trial was over, I was left with too many unanswered questions and I had too much invested emotionally to just let it all go. I was also filled with sympathy for all of the people who were so thoughtlessly hurt by Lori Vallow Daybell's horrific actions.

I knew the story was convoluted and confusing, but what I didn't think about when I started writing my story was how many layers were yet to be peeled off, how many facts were yet to reveal themselves. The most frustrating thing for me has been that as soon as I write about something, new information is exposed. It keeps the story relevant and exciting though.

I know other jurors who served on this trial have gotten back to their lives, but I also know their lives have changed to differing degrees. Some are affected profoundly and are struggling to come to terms with what they were exposed to. Others are back to life as normal, but I'm sure that serving on this jury will never leave them.

It seems like every day we are confronted with horrible crimes. Just watch the news any evening and you see mass shootings and the senseless killing of innocent people. One of the most festering questions I was left with after being subjected to senseless murder firsthand was *why does this happen?* I guess I should have known that at some point it would come into my life in some way.

Any senseless murder is horrific, but to me, murder at the hands of your mother is the most unimaginable and unforgivable of all murders. It's also the hardest for me to understand.

I have been many things in my life, and I have taken on some big challenges, but this one—writing this book—is new to me. I grew up in the '60s and '70s and have the perspective of someone growing up then. Much different than people who missed all of that, the muscle cars and the music of course, but mostly the freedom. Those years were the golden age in our country, as far as I'm concerned, and unfortunately, in my opinion, our country has declined since.

I am a father, husband, grandfather, uncle, nephew, brother, and son. I am fortunate to call a lot of good people my friends. I spent the majority of my productive years as a contractor designing and building custom homes. I've served my community in different ways, including school board, baseball coach, and even scoutmaster for a short time.

I moved my family from Northern California to Idaho in 2005. We started out in small town Idaho in what I would call the Mormon belt. Most of the people in my small town were Mormon and almost all of the businesses and all the schools were run by Mormons. The police were mostly Mormon, the county offices were run by Mormons and the school was run by Mormons. There were other denominations, but the two biggest churches in this small town were Mormon. I say this not as a judgment but because my exposure to the Mormon religion became a factor in my experience of the Lori Vallow Daybell trial.

One of my passions has always been baseball. The first year my family and I lived in this town, it needed an American Legion baseball coach. Since my son had joined the team, I was asked to coach and agreed. I had no idea at the time that my not being Mormon would be a problem. My son had been attending school there long enough to know and he tried to warn me, but I have always been able to break through whatever barriers were between me and the people I was surrounded with, so in spite of his warnings, I decided to give it a go.

Well, the Mormon boys on the team were used to running things and I'll just say we never won a game all season. My inability to get through to them, create some team magic, and make that season a success for the boys, at least on some level, was and always will be a failure of mine.

I'm not blaming it on the fact that they were Mormon, but I am saying that it runs deep. It reminded me of the years I spent coaching Little League Baseball in Northern California. A big percentage of the players there were Native American and lived on what we called the Rancheria. Rancheria is a fancy way of saying poverty-stricken, drug-infested hellhole. I don't think the people who live there and are trying to make it better will be offended by me saying that. They know what it is and are doing their best to improve life there. It's pretty hard to blame the people who live there for what it is. The Native American population in that part of Northern California have had their way of life stripped from them in the same way the Sioux and Cheyenne of the Plains states and the Apache and Comanche of the South have had their way of life stripped from them. Their *foundation*, the ability to live their lives in the way they knew, was lost long ago. Their hunting and fishing grounds are lost, their ability to forage is lost. The land they roamed has been reduced over and over again to what it is now and what it is now is just the Rancheria, a few acres of run-down houses. Packs of feral dogs roam the streets, garbage and broken-down cars and pickups sit in the yards. You can build a big, beautiful house, but if you don't put it on a good foundation, it will inevitably fail.

The people living on the Rancheria have their own trail of tears. As white men encroached on their traditional lands, they were forcibly moved over and over again. Tribes that were at war with each other for hundreds, if not thousands of years, were forced to live together and to this day the animosities between tribes still exist. I and others tried and tried to break through and make life better in some way for our young players, but it was like beating your head against a brick wall. I'm sad to say that some of those kids didn't make it to adulthood, or at least not far into their twenties.

Living in Boise over the last ten years has been healing for me in a way. Boise is more well-rounded as far as religions and ethnicities go, but the dominant religion is still Mormon. I have a lot of Mormon friends here and I have to say I don't have any of the problems I had in the small Idaho town we started out in. I think because that town was so isolated and the Mormons were so powerful there, it was dysfunctional in a way and, as I have since discovered, not typical of all Mormon communities.

My experience with Mormons and Mormon communities led me to be interested in learning about the culture and history of Mormonism and Idaho in general, just as living close to the Rancheria in Northern California sparked my interest in Native American culture and history. Going back in time, the Native American and the Mormon cultures are intertwined. So, in a way, looking back on my experience as a juror in this particular trial, it almost seems to me to be fate.

I give you this personal history only to give you, the reader, an idea of my point of view. I pretty much take religion like skin color. I don't judge anyone based on the color of their skin or their religion. However, if you use your skin color or religion unfairly, I will certainly judge you for that.

Usually I think we can learn from our mistakes or the mistakes of others and go forward with that knowledge. There was none of that in the Lori Daybell trial because there is no way I can understand how a mother and wife can do the things Lori Daybell did. No new laws I can think of to be passed to protect children, no guidance I can think of to give. My experience with the trial was overwhelmingly bad in most regards and it left me wondering what good could possibly come from it. Are there red flags we should be aware of? Is there any way to identify a Lori Daybell, a Charles Manson, or a Jim Jones? Each generation seems to produce its own weird, cultish, dangerous kind of people.

There are, however, still children right now at risk and in danger. Children who unfortunately are born into families, while maybe not as evil as Lori Daybell's, maybe still dangerous or lacking the will or the resources, financial, emotional, or spiritual, to provide for their needs.

This book is not only dedicated to those children, but if I am fortunate enough to write a book people will read, profits from the book will be donated to an organization that exists to help children at risk or in danger, in the hope of getting at least some small good out of the horrible murders of Tylee and JJ.

This book is also dedicated to Tylee and JJ. My hope is that somehow, some way, they will know that some child or some children will experience the peace and security that all children deserve, and that they were so brutally robbed of.

Not to leave out Tammy Daybell and Charles Vallow, the spouses who were murdered in this case. They were as innocent as they could possibly be and certainly didn't deserve what Chad and Lori Daybell and Alex Cox did to them. From all the research I have done on them, I think no one could ask for a better spouse than these two were to their respective spouses.

I feel like there are so many other people who this book should also be dedicated to, so I will at least acknowledge some of them here:

JJ's grandparents, Kay and Larry Woodcock who were generous enough not just to talk to me, but to kind of take me in, after all they have been through. My good friend and a wonderful father, Thomas, who first suggested I write this book, and his two beautiful little twin daughters. My parents who provided us with such a loving, safe home. My beautiful wife Susan who supported me writing this book as she always supports me in everything I attempt. My sister Noreen, who is an attorney and author who helped me format and edit my manuscript. My jury friend Laura, who helped me remember things correctly. Everyone who allowed me to interview them: family members, police, investigators, attorneys, fellow jurors and media people. All of the good people who dedicate themselves to protecting us and seeing justice done and do the hard work every day. They are what got me through this trial intact. Just knowing our communities are full of good people and that evildoers, although they command a lot of our attention, are such a minute percentage. I am truly blessed and overwhelmed by the good people in my life. I am pleasantly surprised to say that this list has grown considerably since my experience as a juror in this trial.

Please note that I use the names Lori Cox, Lori Ryan, Lori Vallow, Lori Vallow Daybell, and Lori Daybell in this book, depending on the time period. She used Vallow when married to Charles and seems to have used Lori Vallow Daybell after ending Charles Vallow's life and marrying Chad Daybell. Her legal name at the time of this writing is Lori Vallow. I don't think she deserves to use the name Vallow after being charged with Charles Vallow's murder, therefore, post Charles, I use Lori Daybell. I apologize to the Daybell family who might not like that, but she is married to Chad Daybell. Although it might be simpler and my writing might have a better flow, I don't want to use just her first name. I think the use of someone's first name indicates a familiarity or personal connection, and I won't give her that honor. And I can't just use her last name because you might confuse her with other people in this story. So, while I know it's confusing, please remember there is only one "Lori" in this story and the name I put after "Lori" refers to the time period I am writing about.

If you are a true crime enthusiast, you will find this book to be different from other true crime books. I do not put the reader through the events as they happened, other than an outline in chapter 3, just for reference. Somebody else will do that. For me it's too close to home and too recent, and I don't want to put you or myself through that.

If you're reading this book in the hope of finding answers to all your questions, you might have to be patient. I hope to answer some of them in this book and plan to follow this book up with another one after the Chad Daybell trial. I am told there will be new evidence, which I hope will answer more of our questions. Sitting through the trial I kept having new questions, a lot of which are still unanswered, even after hours and hours of research. As a juror, you are expected to sit there quietly listening to the testimony. I had to stop myself, more than once, from standing up in frustration and shouting out what seemed to me to be an obvious question.

I guess you can consider this book to be my attempt to make sense of what I was put through as a juror, and share with you what I learned, both factually and emotionally. By the time the trial was over, I was left with so many unanswered questions. The research I have done since the trial ended has answered a lot of them, but the big unanswerable question I think is missed by everyone and we'll ask it in this book. So let's get to it:

PART ONE:
MY EXPERIENCE AS A JUROR

CHAPTER 1:
WAIT, WHAT?
(JURY SELECTION)

When I got the letter in the mail kindly suggesting that I show up for jury duty, I had no idea what the trial would be or how big it was. I still didn't even suspect it when I showed up at the courthouse. I was put in a room with a lot of other people, and I guess I should have had a clue then, but I just thought it was business as usual at the Ada County Courthouse in Boise, Idaho. There were trials to be tried and they needed jurors to try them.

I was given a number. My number was 1864, but I didn't think that meant I was number 1864 out of what someone later said was 2400 total jurors called in for this case. I've heard there were 1800, 2400, and 2600 initial calls out to potential jurors. All three of those numbers came from people I thought should know. Whichever number it was, it was a lot of people called for jury service in this case. Serving on a jury was my duty as a citizen and I would do as they asked.

What they asked of me first was to fill out a questionnaire. It was pretty generic and still didn't clue me in to what I might be in for. That was it for Day One. A few days later, I received a message that I was again to show up at the courthouse at a given time. I showed up and again sat in the same room with a whole bunch of other people. Potential jurors were being called into the courtroom around 50 at a time. Still not having a clue but wondering what case I might be called in for, I waited for my group to be called. Let me tell you, if you haven't experienced it yet, things in the judicial system don't move along very fast.

When I was finally called to go in, I lined up with the rest of the people in my group waiting to be escorted into the courtroom. Here I should say I was only vaguely familiar with Lori Daybell. I knew her kids had been missing for a long time and that they were eventually found dead. I knew what she looked like from news clips that I really didn't pay much attention to. (I know it sounds strange that anyone wouldn't be very familiar with the case, especially someone living in Idaho, but I spent a lot of the Covid years building a cabin in the mountains up close to the continental divide between Idaho and Montana where I had no internet, cell service, or even electricity.) Two bailiffs escorted us into the courtroom and there she was, sitting between her two attorneys! It hit me like a brick in the face. And she was looking right at us.

A lot of emotions were coursing through me at this moment. The first thing I felt as I walked into the courtroom was the weight of the responsibility I would have serving as a juror in this court. I could feel it. It was so quiet you could have heard a pin drop, and there must have been close to 100 people in that courtroom.

After the trial was over, I heard people say they felt pure evil emanating from the defendant. Whether it was something real that actually existed or just an emotion people felt, I'm not sure.

But that first day, there she was, sitting right across from me, and she was looking at each of us in turn. When her eyes came to me, I refused to let myself look away until she did, but man was it hard. I didn't want to look at her. I didn't even want to admit to myself that people who were accused of what she was accused of existed on this earth or that they were real. It's not that I was assuming she was guilty. It was just that people had been murdered and it was sad. Her situation was sad. I hadn't thought about it before, but before that, I guess I just thought of her as someone on TV. Separated from me by that. But not anymore. This was the first time during this trial that I realized I was being confronted with realities I would rather have avoided.

At this point, the judge, Hon. Steven Boyce, announced to us what the case was, so now there could be no doubt—but the reality still hadn't totally sunk in.

My first impression of Judge Boyce, which was reinforced over the next several weeks, was that he was a kind and thoughtful man. Possibly it was because of his position, sitting above us all in his robes, but he seemed fair. He seemed like the kind of person I would want trying my case, if I were on trial. One thing I noticed right away is that he did not have a gavel. I was kind of disappointed by that. I wanted him to have a gavel. I guess maybe it's a thing of the past, but in all the movies I've ever watched there was a gavel and at some point it was used by the judge to bring order in the court.

Judge Boyce was appointed by Idaho Gov. Brad Little in 2019 to the Idaho Seventh Judicial District. He is a member of the LDS Church, as are most people from southeast Idaho. I learned later that some people didn't think he would be up to the task. How could any judge be? This case was so convoluted. I think he did well though. Not just because he was able to wind his way through it all without making any critical mistakes, but also because I think he stood firmly on the law and didn't allow himself to be backed into a corner. There are many decisions a judge has to make daily in a trial like this and any wrong decision can lead to a successful appeal of the verdict.

Still though, there were up to 2600 potential jurors, so what were the chances of me actually sitting on the jury? I calculated the odds in my head while I sat there, something to take my mind off the heaviness of the moment. One chance in 144.4 to be exact. That is using 2600 as the number of potential jurors.

Judge Boyce asked us a lot of questions and we were given the opportunity to say why we shouldn't serve on this jury. It was pretty obvious to me what I should say if I wanted to get out of it. Basically, they were looking for people who were not aware of what had been all over the news in Idaho, and the whole world for that matter, for over two years.

He asked if it was a hardship for anyone and my mind was racing thinking about everything I would have to put off, all of my plans I would have to change to serve for a trial he said might last for eight weeks. By the time he came to me, I had heard some real hardships that some people would be facing if they had to serve on the jury and mine seemed pretty weak. My work is somewhat seasonal and springtime is when I usually start painting, replacing fences, fixing broken sprinkler systems, and things like that. None of it is critical. Putting it off for two months would just mean it would pile up and I would have to catch up later, but I could certainly do that.

One young woman was a single mom of two kids and worked two jobs. She was afraid she would lose her jobs if she had to serve on the jury. At the very least, she would lose the pay she would have received, and she said she would not be able to pay her rent, among other things. Another guy had his own business and was required to travel. He would lose his contracts and the income associated with them. He would have to lay off some of his employees. Judge Boyce did not release either of these people, at least not right then. After hearing these stories and others, I would have been embarrassed to say mine out loud. There went my first opportunity to walk away. I wasn't too concerned though, because my chances of being chosen to serve were still very slim.

Before being released for the day, Judge Boyce admonished us potential jurors, as he would at the end of every day: We were not to talk to anyone about the trial or watch, listen to, or read anything related to the trial. So, not only were we going to be in court every day for up to eight weeks, but we couldn't tell anyone what we were up to.

Eight weeks is a long time and there were people wondering what I was up to. Because this case was so prominent in Idaho, some figured it out on their own, which was fine, and they were curious but respectful when I explained I wasn't able to talk about it. Well, I can talk about it now!

I was called back the next day for mostly the same long, boring drill. This time when my group was called in, the attorneys questioned us individually. The most common question was basically: What do you know about this case? Then: How do you *not* know about this case? Have you watched the series about the case on Netflix?

Like I said earlier, I didn't know much. I was honest when asked how I didn't know much. I just said I found the story depressing and sordid, so I didn't pay attention to it when I saw it on the news. It was true, but I thought the defense might be offended by my answer. Apparently they weren't, or I suspect they were grasping to find 18 jurors who knew as little as I did. As for the prosecution, they told me later they were looking for people who they thought would be able to follow such a complicated case. That was it for Day Three—after the admonishment from Judge Boyce, of course.

Day Four was kind of bizarre and I wasn't exactly sure what was going on. There were 42 of us in the courtroom and I didn't know we had been boiled down to just those 42. Had I known, I would have calculated my chances of serving on the jury at 1 in 2.33. Considerably worse than the 1 in 144.4 of the previous days. The attorneys kept looking at individual jurors and passing papers back and forth, through the bailiff, from the defense to the prosecution and vice versa.

I found out later after the sentencing, when I interviewed the prosecution team, that the prosecution and the defense each had the opportunity to release 12 potential jurors without having to have a reason. They would look over the jury, write something down, and hand it to the bailiff. The bailiff would walk the paper over to the opposing counsel. Opposing counsel would look at it and write something down, hand it to the bailiff, and the bailiff would make a return trip. This took hours and was excruciatingly boring, especially since I had no idea what they were up to.

Finally juror numbers were called out and those jurors whose numbers were called were thanked for their time and dismissed. We were down to 18. I still didn't understand we were the final 18 and I was on the jury! After being admonished by the judge, we left the courtroom and were escorted into the jury room.

Randy, the court's jury administrator, started giving us instructions and it slowly dawned on me. Holy crap, I was on the jury for the Lori Vallow Daybell case! Everyone was kind of looking around at each other, realizing we would be spending a lot of time together, and I imagine wondering where we all stood. According to Judge Boyce's admonition, we couldn't even discuss the trial with each other. I noticed some people had a kind of stunned look on their faces and I imagine I did too.

We were told we would be picked up at an as yet undisclosed location and driven to the courthouse in vans. We would be notified when and where to be, and the pickup location would be changed regularly.

Now I was a little nervous. According to the charges filed against her, Lori Daybell had either murdered or conspired to murder people she knew. Was I in danger? Was my family in danger? Would the pickup location be secure and guarded? Maybe I've watched too many movies. At the time, I didn't know who Alex Cox was or that he was dead. I didn't know who the players were, and I didn't know whether some of them might still be out there. I wouldn't say I was afraid, but I did ask my wife to keep the doors locked when I wasn't home, and to be aware of what was going on around her, something we're not used to in Boise.

Looking back, I realize they were more concerned with the media hunting us down than any danger we might be in. Of course, I wouldn't have talked to a reporter if they had found me, but the court didn't know that for sure and there was a lot at stake. The media did try to contact me after the trial was over, but I didn't answer their calls. I simply didn't answer if the call came from someone not in my contacts. Once I figured out who in the media were legitimate, I talked to those people well after the verdict was in, but even then, I was careful about what I said, not wanting to take the chance of saying something the defense could use in an appeal.

As it turned out, I was right to be careful. One juror innocently said something to Nate Eaton, a reporter who had covered the case extensively since the beginning. Neither the juror nor Nate Eaton would have intentionally done anything to endanger the verdict, but something was said by the juror that the defense tried to use to call for a mistrial. Fortunately that didn't go anywhere, but why take the risk?

We live in a very quiet neighborhood with only one way in and out and only two short streets that both end in cul-de-sacs.

We all know each other and if there is ever a police car or fire truck in the neighborhood it's big news. We started noticing police cars going by regularly or sometimes parked just down the street from our house. I never did find out for sure, but I suspect they were patrolling the neighborhood just to make sure we weren't being harassed. I wasn't sure at the time whether to be reassured by the security, or more nervous.

You're probably wondering why "juror number 18." We all know that according to our U.S. Constitution, a criminal trial jury consists of 12 jurors. In this trial there would be 12 jurors, plus 6 alternates. The kicker was, that no one would know who the 6 alternates were until their number was literally pulled out of a hat after the prosecution and defense rested and the judge gave his instructions to the jury, just before the jury went into deliberations. Judge Boyce told me later they did that because it would be such a long trial and surely some jurors would have to drop out due to health, family, or something. But not one juror did.

I was proud of the other jurors (and myself) for seeing it through to the end. It wasn't easy for any of us, and I think it was very hard for some. Not just because of time away from family and work, but also emotionally. Some of the subject matter we were exposed to was not for the faint of heart. It definitely took a toll on all of us. There were a few who I thought would crack, but they stuck it out.

I had the opportunity to meet with the ones I was concerned about a few weeks after the trial and they seemed okay but are seeing a counselor. I hope they are okay. They are good people and didn't deserve to be confronted with what we had to see and hear in that courtroom. Eighteen more victims of Lori Daybell— although I'm sure my fellow jurors wouldn't admit that.

Talking to some of the other jurors after the trial was over, I found out some of them actually cried when they learned they were on the jury. Not only because of the enormity of the case, but because of the hardship it would cause them serving for up to eight weeks, financially and otherwise. A few were moms with young children at home and I know at least one was a contractor with contracts to keep. Some were shocked and confused as to how they suddenly found themselves on the jury for this case. Some had mixed emotions, being excited to serve as jurors on such an important case, but at the same time feeling the weight of the responsibility.

I know some of the jurors weren't sure if they and their families were safe from Lori Daybell and her "friends." Remember, we didn't know much going into the trial. We didn't know who the people were in the courtroom gallery. For all we knew, the people who were looking us over constantly could have been Lori Daybell's supporters.

At least one of us was followed home by the media during the trial. The idea that someone could do that must have been terribly unnerving. They would have had to follow our jury van from the courthouse to our parking lot, and from there, they would have had to follow the juror home. This was something our drivers were very careful to avoid, so they must have been quite stealthy about it.

The other jurors I talked to after the trial was over all said they felt the police investigating this case did an amazing job. They felt sad the police had to experience the things they had to go through, and their hearts went out to the officers. I know I felt that way.

When I asked one of the other jurors what they thought about the defense not calling any witnesses her response was: "Who could they call?" I thought that was a great answer and I had to agree because it was so true. By the time the kids' bodies were found, Lori and Chad Daybell had lost the support of everyone, even Lori Daybell's mother who had supported her right up until the bodies were found in Chad Daybell's backyard.

I think we jurors universally felt proud of the system we became a part of. I can say for sure I was proud to have served with 17 other people who I feel now were more than up for the task. Of course we all had different personalities, different political views, and different backgrounds, and that is as it should be, but I think we were respectful of each other and worked together well.

After the trial was over, we were offered counseling and I did consider it, and still might take advantage of the offer. We'll see how it goes. I'm hoping writing this book will help set my mind at ease.

I've had some weird dreams and full-on night terrors since the trial, which hadn't happened to me in years. One of the night terrors featured the bat Charles supposedly used to hit Alex in the head. Who knows why; nothing else in the dream made sense. It took me a minute after waking up to realize everything in my world was okay. It did make me terribly sad thinking of the terror Tylee and JJ must have felt.

CHAPTER 2: FOUNDATION

Foundation: *"an underlying base or support."*

We all understand the purpose of a foundation under a structure. It separates the structure from the earth, holds it fast in the wind or an earthquake, and keeps it from sinking into the ground. The foundation of a book is just as important. The foundation of a book is the story and the purpose for telling it.

Serving on this jury, I learned that, in a legal sense, "foundation" is very important. For instance, a witness can't just get on the stand and start talking. Over and over again in this trial, I listened to the defense object to witness testimony based on lack of foundation. "Foundation," in the evidentiary sense, means the witness has personal knowledge of something—observed it, felt it, smelled it. The prosecutor questioning the witness would have to go back and create a foundation for the statement the witness was making, usually in the form of a question. For instance, if the witness said he or she knew something to be true, the defense would object based on a lack of foundation. The prosecuting attorney would then have to go back and ask the witness questions explaining how the witness knew it to be true, or how the witness had the expertise to testify on the topic. It couldn't be just hearsay.

When the defense objected on the grounds of "hearsay," I was confused. It could be a statement made by the person testifying or a statement made by another person to the person testifying. In other words, if the person testifying in court made a statement on the witness stand like: "I told the defendant not to shoot him," or:

"he told the shooter not to shoot him," that could be hearsay. The witness would have had to see, hear, taste, or smell it himself or herself, or have the professional training and experience to answer the question. So, the *foundation* had been laid for the witness' testimony. Are you confused? I have to admit that I still don't quite get it.

The story I have to tell is not a good—or maybe I should say, not a happy—story. Don't get me wrong, there is some good *in* the story; mainly good people, doing what is right. The contrast between the prosecutors, law enforcement, the judge, and the bad actors in the story couldn't be more obvious.

Let me tell you, good and evil are real. If you were in that courtroom, you would have no doubt about that. It's like when you are in the pitch dark and suddenly a bright light is turned on. At that moment, you know the difference between light and dark.

Light and dark play a big part in this story and you will hear more about that.

The setting: The Ada County Courthouse sits in downtown Boise Idaho. Boise is one of the fastest growing cities in the United States, but it's trying to maintain its small-town feel. Boise proper has about 245,000 people. The State of Idaho has 1.9 million residents, so Boise makes up about 1/8 of the total. It's a college town, home to Boise State University. (You may know it by its blue football field.) The college is downtown. You can see the college from upstairs in the courthouse. It sits right on the beautiful Boise River and the Boise River Greenbelt, a 40-mile-long paved path through one park after another, which winds its way through the city. There is little crime in Boise, little graffiti, and one homeless person downtown.

Actually, I know there is more than one homeless person, but that's what you see, and Boise and the State of Idaho do a better job than most cities and states in dealing with the homeless problem. And I don't mean hiding the problem. We deal with it by providing an avenue for improvement and help where assistance is meaningful. In other words, if someone hits hard times and finds himself or herself on the street, there are people and organizations ready and willing to help. They provide shelter, food, clothing, and a list of available jobs. Anyone taking advantage of these services is expected to want a hand up and not just a hand out. Those unwilling to accept a hand up with the condition that they stay clean of drugs and alcohol and work toward bettering their situation are offered counseling and programs to help. Those unwilling to accept that are left with no other option other than to hit the streets and beg for what they need, and those are the few that you see. Boiseans are pretty generous and tolerant so even those few probably do okay, at least until winter hits. It can get pretty cold downtown, even getting down to zero degrees occasionally, and it tends to get windy in the winter. I guess that is as much of a deterrent to homelessness as anything. I'm not making any judgments or opinions, just describing our situation here to you.

It's not a perfect city and some of the problems of the outside world are slowly creeping in. We even had our own mall shooting a few years ago, and as of this writing in early August of 2023 we have already had six police shootings this year. Police shootings used to be extremely rare here. The most alarming thing about this to me is that most of the media here indirectly blame it on the police. Certainly we question and hold the police to a very high standard, but how about writing about the increase in crime that caused those shootings? Why is there more crime? Where is it coming from? What is causing people to be more violent?

Still, Boise is a place where people are generally happy to live and still have a good quality of life that is getting harder and harder to find in the U.S. You can see it in the people here. They are happier and more likely to meet you with an easy smile or slow down to let you turn into traffic. While the weather can be a little harsh, it's not that cold here by Idaho standards and we get very little rain, so overall it's pretty darn nice.

The Ada County Courthouse is home to the Idaho Fourth Judicial District Court. Because it is home to the U.S. District Court for the State of Idaho, it is a federal building, and you have to go through security to get in, similar to what you experience at the airport except the people providing the security seem happier.

You see all types of people walking through the ground floor of the courthouse, including a lot who look like they must be criminal defendants of some kind or other. We were spared all of this during the trial because we were brought in through a different entrance.

The reason the trial was held in Ada County is that there was likely no way to find an impartial jury in Fremont or Madison Counties where the crimes were committed, so Judge Boyce allowed a change of venue. The upcoming Chad Daybell trial is scheduled to be in Boise also, although the prosecution team is trying to get it switched back to Fremont County where the alleged crimes were committed.

I said before that we were picked up at a parking lot in another part of town. We were driven to the courthouse by our two security guards, Steve and Ken. They were also the bailiffs for the trial. Both were awesome people and I actually miss seeing them since the trial ended. They were with us all day and did everything they could to make us comfortable, including being lighthearted, even though you could tell they had a ton of responsibility. They would go out of their way to fill some minor request of a juror, but their main responsibility was to keep us separated from the media or anyone else who might want to get to us. And it was shocking how some in the media would break the rules and attempt to make contact with us. As I said before, they followed our vans trying to find out where we were parked and even showed up at a juror's home.

One day after leaving court in our van, our driver, Ken, accidentally turned the wrong way on a one-way street trying to lose someone who was following us. We all got a tense laugh out of that at Ken's expense. I have to say though, I don't think any of the people trying to follow us were mainstream media. More like bloggers; people trying to make a name for themselves at the cost of a potential mistrial. Most of the media were very respectful.

Two reporters, Justin Lum from Arizona and Nate Eaton from Idaho, are top notch reporters and were on this story from the beginning. Since the trial ended and in preparation for this book, I have read everything I can find that they have written about this case.

In this book I also use information gained from Lauren and Dr. John Matthias and their podcast, "Hidden: A True Crime

Podcast," as well as information from Gigi McKelvey's podcast, "Pretty Lies and Alibis." I had the privilege of meeting and talking to Lauren and Gigi at the sentencing; they are awesome and full of information about this case.

After being picked up at our "undisclosed" location and driven across town, we were driven through a roll-up door into the basement of the courthouse where two more guards were waiting for us. We were escorted to our impossibly small jury room. At least we had a window with a nice view to the north where we could watch the weather improve as the season changed from winter to spring, and the snowline receded up the mountains. If you knew me, you would know it was torture for me being cooped up in a small room with a bunch of people not of my choosing. It brought back memories of my childhood, being in school stuck in class desperately wanting to be outside. It also reminded me of the 1957 movie *Twelve Angry Men,* starring Henry Fonda. I guess that was before women were allowed to serve on juries. We had an even mix of men and women on our jury.

Once in the jury room, we spent from a half hour to an hour waiting to be called into court, depending on what was going on inside the courtroom. I have since learned that the attorneys argued a lot about what the jury could and could not be exposed to, and I guess that's why we had to wait so long on some mornings.

Finally, our guard, Ken, would come and let us know it was time to go in. He would open the door to the courtroom, say "all rise," and we would go to our seats. Always the same seat. They were numbered.

Lori Daybell would be sitting in front of us between her two defense attorneys, John Thomas and Jim Archibald. More to be said about those two guys later.

There were four prosecutors representing the State: Lindsey Blake, Rob Wood, Rachael Smith, and Spencer Rammell. More about them later, too. Both sides had people in the courtroom supporting them.

The judge, Hon. Steven Boyce, sat at his bench above us all, along with two clerks. Other staff members that were with us daily included the court reporter (who can say how they do what they do?); a security guard at each door, one in the front and one in the back of the courtroom; the bailiff, roaming around doing errands; two plainclothes security officers sitting directly behind Lori Daybell; and another clerk. I think she was in charge of the audio and video feed going into the overflow room.

The gallery was probably the most interesting. I have to admit I spent some time looking at the people in the gallery, trying to figure out who they might be. A lot of them turned out to be people involved in the case—detectives, FBI, prior friends of the defendant, etc. A lot were media, of course. An older man was always there, and I thought he looked familiar. He turned out to be JJ's grandfather, Larry Woodcock. I can only assume this has been as hard on him as anyone, and I hope the verdict and sentence gave him at least some level of peace. His wife, JJ's grandmother, Kay Woodcock, was not able to sit with him in the courtroom gallery because she would be called on as a witness.

I have a lot to say about some of the above-mentioned people in later chapters. Some are my heroes, some I wonder whether they will face charges later. I want to mention Rexburg Detective Ray Hermosillo here. He was the case agent, and he was there from the first day of jury selection all the way to the verdict. I think he best represents the people who devoted their lives to getting the verdict we got.

No cameras were allowed in the courtroom. Judge Boyce nixed that at one of the many pretrial hearings, because, as he said, Lori Daybell would play up to the cameras. Cell phones and laptops were allowed, but they weren't to be visible, and no pictures were to be taken.

So that kind of sets the scene. A big courtroom, but pretty conventional otherwise. Probably pretty close to whatever vision you have in your mind. A ton of security and about 100 people in the gallery. The most distinctive element of course was Lori Daybell. Even though, as far as I could tell, she had no one in court to support her. No family, no friends, nobody but those who were called in to testify against her. As much as you would not want it to, everything had to and did center around her. The star of her show. Too bad it was a horror show.

CHAPTER 3:
A BRIEF OVERVIEW
OF WHAT SHE DID

You're probably familiar with what Lori Daybell did. After all, it has been all over the news, Netflix, Fox Nation, *Dateline*, *48 Hours*, Newsnation, Hidden: A True Crime Podcast, etc. but I want to give you an overview just in case, and from that we'll dive deeper into the victims, perpetrators, police, religion, and maybe more.

Dates weren't that important to me, but it all started around 2018, at least as it relates to this trial, and it won't be over until Chad Daybell's trial is finished. Or until the family finally gets to lay JJ and Tylee to rest. I just heard yesterday that Judge Boyce released JJ's body to his next of kin. I guess that would be Kay and Larry Woodcock. I hope I get to be there when they lay him to rest. I would like the opportunity to support the family and honor JJ.

Chad Daybell's trial commenced on April 1, 2024. He could have pleaded out to avoid the death penalty, but he chose to put everyone through an extremely long and expensive trial, not only in terms of dollars, but emotionally as well. The sequence of events is a little confusing. Here is a cast of characters and a timeline to help you keep things straight:

Characters

Charles Vallow: Lori Vallow Daybell's ex-husband, number 4, deceased

Joe Ryan: Lori Vallow Daybell's ex-husband, number 3, deceased

Chad Daybell: Lori Vallow Daybell's husband, number 5, in jail awaiting trial

Tammy Daybell: Chad Daybell's first wife, deceased

7 year old Joshua Jackson (JJ) Vallow: Lori Vallow Daybell and Charles Vallow's adopted son, deceased

16 year old Tylee Ryan: Lori Vallow Daybell's daughter with Joe Ryan, Charles Vallow's adopted daughter, Joe Ryan's daughter, deceased

Colby Ryan: Lori Vallow Daybell's son, Joe Ryan's stepson, Charles Vallow's adopted son

Melani Boudreaux (now Pawlowski): Lori Vallow Daybell's niece

Brandon Boudreaux: Melani Boudreaux's ex-husband

Summer Shiflet: Lori Vallow Daybell's sister

Kay Vallow Woodcock: Charles Vallow's sister, JJ's grandmother

Larry Woodcock: Kay's husband, JJ's grandfather

Alex Cox: Lori Vallow Daybell's brother, uncle of JJ and Tylee, Zulema Pastenes' husband, deceased

Barry and Janice Cox: Lori Vallow Daybell and Alex Cox's parents

Zulema Pastenes: Alex's wife, in Lori and Chad Daybell's inner circle

Samantha Gwilliam: Tammy Daybell's sister

Garth Daybell: Chad and Tammy Daybell's son

Melanie Gibb: Lori Vallow Daybell's best friend

David Warwick: Melanie Gibb's husband

Audrey Barattiero: Lori Vallow Daybell's friend, part of her inner circle

Julie Rowe: Chad Daybell's friend and author

Megan Conner: Lori Vallow Daybell's cousin

Stacey Cox: Lori Vallow Daybell's sister, deceased. Melani Boudreaux's mother

Heather Daybell: Chad Daybell's sister-in-law

Timeline:

1990: Chad and Tammy Daybell marry.

2006: Lori Ryan marries Charles Vallow.

2008: Lori Vallow's niece, Melani Pawlowski, marries Brandon Boudreaux.

2014: Charles and Lori Vallow adopt JJ, move to Kauai, Hawaii, move back to Arizona.

2015: Chad and Tammy Daybell move to Salem, Idaho.

April 3, 2018: Tylee's father, Joseph Ryan, dies of a supposed heart attack.

Fall 2018: Lori Vallow and Melani Pawlowski begin attending prepper meetings. (I explain what a "prepper" is later on in the book, but basically a group of people preparing for the second coming of Christ.)

October 26, 2018: Lori Vallow meets Chad Daybell at a religious conference in St. George, Utah.

October 28, 2018: Lori Vallow creates a phone contact in her phone for Chad Daybell labeled "Bishop Shumway."

November, 2018: Chad Daybell attends a conference in Arizona and stays at Lori Vallow's house while her husband, Charles, is away. Chad Daybell and Lori Vallow secretly "seal" themselves in the Mormon Church. *(To be "sealed" in the Mormon Church means together as man and wife, as sanctioned by the Mormon Church, for eternity. This particular "sealing" was not sanctioned by the Mormon Church.)*

December 5, 2018: Chad Daybell and Lori Vallow appear together on a podcast they call "Time to Warrior Up."

January, 2019: Lori Vallow tells Melanie Gibb that Charles is taken over by an evil spirit.

January 31, 2019: Body camera footage from the Chandler, AZ Police Dept. showing Charles saying Lori Vallow needs to be committed.

February, 2019: Charles files for divorce from Lori Vallow. Charles changes the beneficiary on his $1 million life insurance policy from Lori Vallow to Kay Woodcock.

April, 2019: Lori Vallow moves to Texas to live with Charles and JJ. Charles halts divorce proceedings.

May 5-7, 2019: Chad Daybell and Lori Vallow both search eBay for malachite rings.

May 17, 2019: Last time Larry and Kay Woodcock see JJ.

June 2019: Lori and Charles Vallow move to Chandler, AZ. Melani Pawlowski and Brandon Boudreaux decide to divorce. Melani claims she received a revelation from God that she wasn't safe with him. Brandon claims she is in a cult with Lori Vallow.

July 1, 2019: Charles tells Lori Vallow he is going to tell Tammy about Lori Vallow's affair with Chad Daybell.

July 11, 2019: Alex Cox shoots and kills Charles Vallow claiming self-defense.

July 12, 2019: Chad Daybell contacts Valley of the Sun Mortuary asking about the price of cremation and sending Charles' cremains to Louisiana.

July 18, 2019: Lori Vallow finds out she is not the beneficiary of Charles' life insurance. She says it's a spear through her heart.

July 20, 2019: Lori Vallow pays for Chad Daybell's flight to Arizona.

July 22, 2019: Lori Vallow and Chad Daybell text each other about Kauai and "the plan."

July 2019: Lori Vallow organizes a casting for Brandon Boudreaux, saying he had an evil spirit, and he was part of Hitler's group and considered "very high dark." *(Note: I explain Chad Daybell's light and dark scale later in this book.)*

August 10, 2019: Kay Woodcock's last conversation with JJ.

August 14, 2019: Lori Vallow applies for townhouse in Rexburg.

August 20, 2019: Lori Vallow moves Tylee's Social Security death benefit that Tylee was receiving for the death of her father, Joe Ryan, to a joint bank account giving herself access to the money.

August 31, 2019: Lori Vallow, Tylee, JJ, Alex, and Melani Pawlowski move to Rexburg.

September 3, 2019: Lori Vallow enrolls JJ at Kennedy Elementary School in Rexburg.

September 8, 2019: Chad and Tammy Daybell apply to increase Tammy's life insurance. Last picture of Tylee alive taken in Yellowstone.

September 9, 2019: Chad Daybell texts Tammy to tell her he shot a raccoon and buried it in the pet cemetery. Phone records later show Alex Cox was at the location of Tylee's gravesite in Chad Daybell's backyard at this time, indicating that Chad Daybell and Alex may have been together at the time Tylee was buried.

September 10, 2019: Lori Vallow deposits Tylee's benefits into the joint bank account.

Mid-September, 2019: Lori Vallow tells Zulema Pastenes that Tylee had to be freed. When questioned by Zulema as to what she meant, Lori Vallow said, "don't ask."

September 18, 2019: Social Security payments for Tylee and JJ were deposited. Lori Vallow interviews Sydney, JJ's babysitter, and lies to her saying JJ's dad died of a heart attack.

September 19, 2019: Lori Vallow tells the babysitter JJ went to his grandparents and the babysitter will no longer be needed. Lori Vallow no longer responds to the babysitter's texts.

September 20, 2019: Last day JJ attends school.

September 22, 2019: Melanie Gibb and David Warwick are staying with Lori Vallow and see Alex take JJ upstairs. JJ was never seen alive after that. The last "proof of life" for JJ was a picture of him sitting on the couch in his red pajamas on this date, the same pajamas he was wearing when police found his body buried in Chad Daybell's backyard.

September 24, 2019: Lori Vallow emails Kennedy Elementary School telling the school JJ has moved to live with his grandparents who will be homeschooling him.

September 30, 2019: Lori Vallow searched the internet for "how to get the back seat out of a Jeep Wrangler."

October 1, 2019: Lori Vallow rents storage unit. Alex is seen many times visiting the storage unit and one time had someone with him who I think might have been Chad Daybell.

October 2, 2019: Brandon Boudreaux is shot at with a rifle sticking out of the back window of a Jeep Wrangler that fits the description of Tylee's Jeep. Gilbert, AZ police first contact to Rexburg, ID police asking for help finding the Jeep. Lori Vallow purchases a wedding ring on Amazon.

October 9, 2019: Tammy calls 911 to report someone shot at her with a paintball gun. In court the prosecution claimed it was actually Alex Cox with an AK type rifle.

October 19, 2019: Chad calls 911 to report Tammy's death. Lori Vallow tells Melanie Gibb Tammy was possessed and they had to get the spirit out of her. She also told Gibb Tammy was getting suspicious of her and Chad Daybell's affair and had "turned dark."

October 22, 2019: Tammy is buried at Evergreen Cemetery in Springville, Utah.

October 23, 2019: Lori Vallow searches the web for "wedding dresses in Kauai."

October 26, 2019: Chad Daybell tells friends he has found the woman he is going to marry. Later Lori Vallow tells friends that her husband died of a heart attack and her daughter died of cancer. Both were lies.

November 4, 2019: Tylee's Jeep seized by Rexburg police.

November 5, 2019: Chad Daybell and Lori Vallow get married on a beach in Kauai.

November 7, 2019: When asked, Lori Daybell tells Zulema Pastenes that JJ is with his grandparents.

November 18, 2019: Kay Woodcock hacks into Charles' Gmail account and finds Lori Daybell's address in Rexburg. She hadn't known Lori Daybell had moved to Rexburg or that she had married Chad Daybell. Kay had become suspicious and worried, and contacted a private investigator to help find JJ.

November 24, 2019: Chad Daybell gives Alex a "patriarchal" blessing. Alex goes quiet after this.

November 25, 2019: Gilbert Police contact Rexburg police about a missing child.

November 26, 2019: Rexburg police conduct a welfare check at the Rexburg apartment looking for JJ. JJ is not there, but Alex and Chad Daybell are seen outside. Detective Hermosillo questions them and becomes suspicious.

November 27, 2019: Rexburg police are granted a search warrant and search Lori Daybell's apartment. It is nearly empty. They find guns, ammo, duct tape, and other incriminating items in the garage. They also find a receipt for the storage unit.

November 29, 2019: Alex Cox and Zulema Pastenes get married in Las Vegas.

December 1, 2019: Chad and Lori Daybell fly to Hawaii and apply for a rental stating they have no kids.

December 6, 2019: Melanie Gibb contacts Rexburg police to tell them Lori Daybell asked her to lie about JJ's location.

December 11, 2019: Fremont County Sheriff's Office exhumes Tammy Daybell's body. The medical examiner determines her death was murder by asphyxiation. Alex tells Zulema where he has hidden money and that "I think I am being their fall guy." He is referring to Chad and Lori Daybell.

December 12, 2019: Alex dies allegedly of natural causes.

December 20, 2019: Rexburg police officially announce JJ and Tylee are missing.

December 21, 2019: Rexburg police declare Chad and Lori Daybell are "persons of interest."

January 3, 2020: Police search Chad Daybell's house and recover several items which they share with the FBI, now involved in the case.

January 7, 2020: Kay and Larry Woodcock announce a $20,000 reward for information leading to the recovery of JJ and Tylee.

January 25, 2020: Kauai police serve Lori Daybell with notice to produce Tylee and JJ within 5 days.

January 26, 2020: Nate Eaton confronts Chad and Lori Daybell in Hawaii asking where the kids are. They don't respond.

January 30, 2020: Lori Daybell misses the deadline to produce her kids.

February 20, 2020: Kauai police arrest Lori Daybell on a $5 million warrant from Madison County. She is charged with two counts of desertion and nonsupport of dependent children, resisting officers, criminal solicitation, and contempt of court.

February 26, 2020: Lori Daybell waives her extradition to Idaho after six days in the Kauai jail.

March 5, 2020: Lori Daybell extradited to Rexburg.

March 6, 2020: Lori Daybell's first court appearance. She was unable to post her $1 million bail and would remain in jail.

April 9, 2020: Idaho Attorney General's office tells East Idaho News Chad and Lori Daybell are under investigation for conspiracy to commit murder, attempted murder, and murder.

May 8, 2020: Alex Cox's autopsy results say that he died of natural causes—blood clots in his lungs.

June 9, 2020: Police find JJ and Tylee's remains on Chad Daybell's property. Chad Daybell transfers money to his kids. He is arrested.

June 10, 2020: Chad Daybell makes his first court appearance. His bail is set at $1 million.

June 8, 2021: Lori Daybell is committed to the Idaho Department of Health and Welfare where she is deemed to be unfit for trial.

April 11, 2022: Lori Daybell is deemed fit for trial.

October 6, 2022: Lori Daybell again found unfit for trial; trial postponed to April 3, 2023.

April 3-7, 2023: Jury selection.

April 10, 2023: Opening statements are given and the trial begins.

May 12, 2023: After deliberating for seven hours, the jury finds Lori Daybell guilty on all charges: two counts of murder, three counts of conspiracy to commit murder, and grand theft.

July 31, 2023: Lori Daybell is sentenced to five life sentences with no chance of parole.

In court we heard testimony from witness Melanie Gibb. Gibb said that Lori Vallow met Chad Daybell in 2018 at a "Preparing a People" conference. "Preparing a People" was a "prepper" group, preparing for the end of times or the second coming of Christ, and not in any way sanctioned by the Mormon Church, although most of the people attending were Mormon. Gibb testified Chad

Daybell was an author of several books and a speaker at the conference. According to Melanie, Chad Daybell and Lori Vallow quickly fell in love in spite of the fact that they were both married to other people and had children with those people. A lot more on all of this later.

I was surprised to learn Lori Vallow Daybell had been married four times at this point. Her first two marriages didn't last long; fortunately her first two husbands seem to have survived. Lucky guys!

Her third husband, Joe Ryan, was her son Colby's stepfather and her daughter Tylee's father. Lori Daybell's son, Colby, later testified in court that Joe Ryan abused him when he was a child. We heard how Lori Daybell's brother Alex used a stun gun on Joe Ryan, threatened to kill him, and served three months in a Texas prison for it. Brother Alex was a stand-up comedian and used this incident in his skits, saying he wasn't sorry for what he did. He did it to protect his sister. Joe Ryan later died of allegedly natural causes.

Charles Vallow was described by Colby on the witness stand as having a business of his own and a good, stable income, which must have been a draw for Lori Ryan. Charles Vallow and Lori Ryan married and lived happily together for several years. Colby came to think of Charles as his father. In fact, when Colby was on the stand he said Charles was the only father figure he ever had.

In 2019, Charles went on a business trip. By this time the marriage was not going well, and Lori Vallow wanted a divorce. While on this trip, Lori Vallow changed the locks on their house in Arizona, emptied $35,000 out of Charles' business account, and removed his car from the airport parking lot. Charles called the police when he got home and couldn't get into his house. He explained to the police that Lori Vallow had threatened to murder him, and he thought she was serious. In court, we watched a video of Charles telling police that Lori Vallow had decided his body was taken over by a zombie called Ned Snyder and that Ned needed to be killed. Charles also reported Lori Vallow had said threatening things about their two kids, Tylee and JJ.

According to Gilbert, Arizona Detective Ryan Pillar's testimony, the police in Arizona took him seriously, but there wasn't much they could do. Before police caught up with Lori Vallow, she voluntarily committed herself to a counseling center, preempting being committed by the police. She was released after only a few hours. I suppose she used her charms and manipulative skills to fool the psychologists who were evaluating her, and I guess she must have somehow known the police were looking for her and were going to have her committed for evaluation.

After moving back to Arizona, following a few years of living in Kauai, Charles and Lori Vallow separated and Charles provided Lori Vallow with her own house for her and her kids to live in. According to Tylee's statement to police taken later that day, there had been a heated argument between Charles and Lori Vallow at Lori Vallow's house when Charles showed up the morning of July 11, 2019 to pick up JJ and take him to school. It had been months since Charles was able to see JJ and he had set up this date, excited to finally reconnect with JJ. Tylee and Lori Vallow were there when Charles got there, but so was Lori Vallow's brother, Alex Cox. JJ was out in the car strapped into his car seat, waiting to be taken to school. Alex claimed that he spent the night at Lori Vallow's request, because she claimed she needed protection from Charles. Allegedly Charles had been threatening Lori Vallow. I wasn't convinced of this while listening to testimony. I knew nothing about Charles, other than what I had learned so far in court. From what I have learned about him since, I very much doubt that Charles was in any way threatening to Lori Vallow.

That July 11, 2019 morning Charles arrived to pick up JJ. Lori Vallow's 16-year-old daughter Tylee was allegedly awakened by yelling and came out of her room with a baseball bat. Charles allegedly took the bat away from Tylee and allegedly came after Alex who was trying to calm Charles down. Alex ended up shooting Charles twice "in self-defense" and Charles died.

The main problem with Alex's self-defense argument was that there was a bullet in the floor underneath Charles' dead body. Alex's second shot into Charles' body appeared to be made after Charles was laying on his back on the floor already having been shot in the chest once at close range with a .45 caliber bullet. Also, Alex Cox's and Lori Vallow's stories to the police later that morning didn't exactly line up. Immediately after Alex shot Charles, Lori Vallow, JJ, and Tylee went off to buy flip flops, stop off at Burger King, and drop JJ off at school.

At the time, after interviewing Alex Cox, Lori Vallow, and Tylee when they came back after dropping JJ off at school, the police in Arizona seem to have bought the story, in spite of contradictions and inconsistencies. Alex Cox and Lori Vallow were, very unfortunately, free to continue on.

Later, on October 9, 2019, back in Rexburg, Chad's wife Tammy was shot at either with a paintball gun or an AK-type rifle. The prosecution tried hard to convince us that it was a rifle. They even brought the rifle into court, I guess thinking that would impress the jury. We all live in Idaho and aren't that impressed with seeing a gun. I was personally left feeling like it probably was an attempted murder using that rifle, but I really didn't feel like the prosecution proved it.

Tammy was supposedly shot at, at least twice, from a short distance away, while exiting her car. It was dark out and Tammy told police she was lifting the groceries she had just bought out of the back seat of her car when she was approached and shot at by a man or teenager, she thought. My thought was the police must have looked for casings or bullets, maybe in the houses or trees across the street, but they never addressed that in court. This is one of many questions I was left hanging with.

I did hear a recording of Tammy's 911 call and I could hear Chad in the background. It sounded like he was in Tammy's ear saying something about a paintball gun. Was he telling her what to say? Why didn't he make the call? Why wasn't he out looking for the shooter? As a husband, I would have been doing all those things.

The prosecution did show that Alex had bought camo gear and other similar items at the local Sportsman's Warehouse just before the shooting took place. They did have a witness, a neighbor across the street, describe the shooter as wearing exactly what Alex had bought. While circumstantial, it was close enough for me, especially because Tammy ended up dead in her bed a few weeks later.

We listened as the prosecution questioned Rexburg Detective Allie Greenhalgh about the morning of October 19, 2019 when she was called to the Daybell residence. The 911 call was placed by Daybell's son Garth, but Chad Daybell took over the call giving his address and saying his wife was clearly dead. We could hear him crying as they played the tape of the call-in court. Detective Greenhalgh said that, when she arrived at the house, Chad Daybell seemed distraught as he described how his wife, Tammy, had been sick the night before coughing and vomiting. He explained she did not like going to doctors and preferred to treat herself at home. According to Chad Daybell, he awoke later the next morning to find her unconscious with her upper torso hanging out of the bed. We were shown pictures taken by the police that morning. Tammy was lying on the bed with pink foam coming out of her mouth.

Initially, Tammy's death was ruled by the coroner as being from natural causes. They had no reason to think foul play might have been at work. However, Tammy's body was exhumed later on December 11, 2019, after the police had become suspicious, and an autopsy was performed by a medical examiner. The medical examiner determined the coroner's determination was incorrect and Tammy's cause of death was homicide by asphyxiation.

In court they showed us pictures of Tammy lying dead in her bed as the medical examiner, Dr. Erik Christensen, Utah's chief medical examiner, testified about his findings after exhuming her body. We also saw pictures of her body after it had been exhumed. The medical examiner used a laser pointer to point out the bruising on her arms. He had cut sections of the bruises and examined them and we were shown pictures of those sections. He determined that they happened around the time of her death, which led him to determine she had been held down by someone.

My thought at the time, looking at the pictures of the bruises, was there must have been more than one person holding her down or there would have been more bruising. She would have been able to put up more of a fight. The only bruising I was able to see on Tammy was on her upper arms and it wasn't much. It looked like the typical bruising one might get bumping into the corner of a cabinet or something like that. There didn't appear to be any bruising on her legs or anywhere else on her body. Still, he proved his point. Tammy had been murdered, but I was left with another one of those lingering questions: Who all was involved and present at her murder? We know, according to FBI testimony, Alex's phone was only a few blocks away at the time of the murder and it was in the middle of the night.

So, Chad Daybell and Lori Vallow were now free to pursue their romance in the open and in fact they got married on a beach in Kauai just two weeks later!

But were they free enough? Apparently not. Brandon Boudreaux, the ex-husband of Lori Vallow's niece, Melani

Boudreaux, was shot at later in Arizona, so they must have felt they needed Brandon out of the way too. Or was Melani involved and willing to kill to get what she wanted? Melani would have been the beneficiary of Brandon's life insurance, and she was a part of Lori and Chad Daybell's inner circle. She was involved in their prepper group and did podcasts with them.

This event, along with Kay and Larry Woodcock contacting the police and media, is actually what spurred the whole investigation in Rexburg that led to the search for JJ and Tylee. A Jeep was spotted by Brandon just as a rifle was pointed out the back window and a shot rang out, shattering his driver side window. He didn't know it was Tylee's Jeep at the time, but he reported a description of the Jeep to Arizona police, and they found out it was registered to Charles Vallow in Texas. Arizona contacted Rexburg police asking them for help locating the Jeep, which led to Detective Hermosillo going to Lori Daybell's apartment in Rexburg and coming in contact for the first time with Chad Daybell.

Who knows if it was Melani who was behind the attempted murder of Brandon, but I'm wondering if there may be other people charged in this case. Fortunately, it was a failed attempt and Brandon was alive to testify in court. It was a close call for Brandon though.

Just before the attempted murder of Brandon, Lori Vallow moved to Rexburg, along with Tylee, JJ, and Lori's brother, Alex. Lori Vallow and Alex Cox each rented an apartment at the same complex in Rexburg. Melani Boudreaux also moved to the same complex.

Lori Vallow contacted Charles' life insurance carrier, assuming she was about to collect $1 million, and found out Charles had removed her from the policy. He had changed the beneficiary to Kay Woodcock. Kay was Charles' sister and JJ's grandmother.

Lori Vallow thought she would get $1 million from Charles' death, but she got nothing. Meanwhile, where are Tylee and JJ?

Grandparents Larry and Kay Woodcock wanted to know. They had always been in close contact with the kids and by now it had been months since they had seen or heard from either one. They were used to FaceTiming with JJ daily, and Lori Vallow refused to tell them why they couldn't do that anymore.

Kay and Larry were like bulldogs, never giving an inch. It all started with their determination to find JJ and Tylee and evolved into their determination to see justice served.

Kay called the police. The police came to Lori Vallow's apartment complex in Rexburg and had their first encounter with Lori (now) Daybell. This was Detective Hermosillo's first encounter with Lori Daybell. On the witness stand, Hermosillo told us how she had lied to him then and continued to lie about where the kids were. He knew she was lying not only from his experience in questioning people, but also because she kept changing her story. She first said they were with Melanie Gibb at the movies watching *Frozen* and later said they were with their grandmother Kay. Lori Daybell also asked Melanie to lie to the police. Melanie actually recorded a phone call she got from Lori Daybell asking her to lie and we heard that in court. The police caught Lori Daybell in several lies and were buying none of them, but still, they didn't know and, according to Detective Hermosillo, they still had hope of finding the kids alive somewhere.

Possibly stashed away on some compound somewhere. Plausible considering preppers tend to not trust any form of government.

The police next find Chad and Lori Daybell in Kauai and serve Lori Daybell with a warrant to produce both children. We were shown a video of this event in court, and I noticed something in it that, although I didn't know it at the time, would be one of the keys to unfolding the mystery of how a mother could kill her children. Lori Daybell was laying back on a lounge chair by a pool, and on the lounge chair by her leg was a book. The title of the book could be plainly seen. It was *Visions of Glory*. When I saw the book, I assumed it was a religious book and I thought it was interesting because it gave me an indication that Lori Daybell was a religious person. Religious enough to read a religious book while on vacation in Hawaii. I found out later it was much more significant than that.

We were shown a video of reporter Nate Eaton in Kauai trying to get Lori Daybell to tell where the children were. Lori and Chad Daybell just ignored Mr. Eaton and continued on their way—apparently to go lay in the sun on the beach without a care in the world.

Eventually, the police would find JJ and Tylee buried in Chad Daybell's backyard!

Right after Tammy's death, Alex died supposedly of natural causes, but he was cremated so who really knows. There are plenty of hard to believe things associated with this trial, but this one is way too much of a coincidence for me to accept.

Okay, so a lot of other things happened during all of what I listed above, and I talk a lot more about all of this later chapters, but this gives you an idea of what we'll be talking about in the rest of this book.

CHAPTER 4:
JUSTICE

What is justice? Why is it so important? Justice is the foundation to our freedom. Just like the foundation of a building, it is a system composed of many parts. Each part, just like the bricks or stones under a structure, serves an important purpose. If one part fails, the whole system fails. Take the keystone out of a stone arch. The arch crumbles, and as it crumbles, everything above it crumbles. The whole building above it depends on that arch in the foundation, and without that arch, the whole building comes down.

Without a good, solid, and equal justice system our whole country will crumble, and just as a building crumbling might start slowly, once it starts coming down, it happens quickly and there is no way to stop it. That's the terrifying part about what I see happening in our country. We are beginning to crumble and maybe we can take quick action and save ourselves, but at some point it will be too late. Once it's too late, what will we be left with? A pile of worthless rubble?

Our system of justice in this country is basically unchanged since our forefathers set it up in the 1700s. They took the system they were familiar with, the British model, and tweaked it to make it more just. More equal and fair to the common man. All defendants are considered innocent until proven guilty. Defendants have the right to a speedy trial and will be judged by their peers. Defendants do not have to incriminate themselves, and so on.

But here we are in 2023 and I think a lot of us question whether the system is broken. Every night on the news we see criminals running free in the streets burning, looting, and fighting with police. We see politicians get away with all kinds of things that we, as citizens, would never get away with. We see crimes committed by criminals with records that should have kept them in jail. Our system of justice is the foundation to the freedom we love, and if the system is broken, boy, are we in trouble?

I want to say here just for the sake of a sociological debate, our sense of justice evolving in our country is not by itself a bad thing. It does, however, take us away from the solutions to crime. Our sense of justice in the past was more of a deterrent to crime.

Many people, like Dr. John Matthais of the Hidden: A True Crime Podcast, have studied and strived to understand what motivates people to commit crimes. I don't know where he stands on this topic, but I believe that understanding why people commit crimes leads us, as a society, to excuse them for it. Some believe going easy on them, maybe giving them a second chance, may be more just for the perpetrators, but in my experience, letting them off easy just leads to more crime. Freeing perpetrators to commit more crimes doesn't help rehabilitate them, it just reinforces bad behavior.

Think of it this way: In the old west, if you committed a crime, you were charged, tried, and punished quickly. If you were convicted of murder, you were more than likely hanged in the town square the next day while everyone watched. However you feel about that, it *is* more of a deterrent to crime.

Interestingly, the state of Idaho just passed a law allowing the use of a firing squad in death penalty cases in the event the drugs used in lethal injection are unavailable. Whatever your position on the death penalty, at least Idaho is trying to promote justice. It has been 11 years since Idaho put anyone to death though and plenty of time is allowed for appeals. So, I think, at least in regard to the death penalty, Idaho is struggling to find the best way to protect the public and also promote closure for not only the victims, but also the person convicted of a crime that put him or her in a position to receive the death penalty. It's a controversial subject for sure, and during the trial I was kind of glad I wasn't put into a position to have to come to terms with it personally.

Somehow, my mind wouldn't let me off that easily. It's one of those lingering thoughts I keep having since the trial ended, one of the unanswered questions. Is it better to put someone like Lori Daybell to death? Is it more just? Would it be easier for her to have been given a death sentence? Would it cause her to more quickly come to terms with what she did? Would it have forced her to ask for forgiveness? Or, might it be more like revenge? Should revenge be part of the conversation? I would bet that the living victims would like it to be. Is the death penalty more of a deterrent to would-be criminals? This question I can answer for myself. Yes, it would be more of a deterrent. It's hardwired into us not to want to die. Even people like Lori Daybell who think they want to die in order to get to heaven faster, when confronted with their death, will do anything to keep it from happening. So, while I don't think it would have been easier for her to have received a death sentence in that regard, I do think she might suffer a lot for as long as she does live.

Anyway, after going around and around in my mind, I have come to a conclusion that I can live with. It's just one person's opinion and I respect your right to have a differing opinion if you do. My opinion is that doing away with the death penalty— and I might as well throw hard labor in too—and guaranteeing food, shelter, and a bed to people who commit heinous crimes like murder, causes more harm than getting tough on them. I think that swift and severe justice in the case of murderers, and hard labor for lesser offenses, while harder on the people who commit those crimes, would be more of a deterrent, and in effect, cause there to be *fewer perpetrators* of crime and *fewer victims* for the perpetrators.

The arguments against this of course are that we are likely to commit people to death wrongfully, possibly putting someone to death who is actually innocent; or that we simple humans don't have the right to take someone's life no matter what the reason.

Putting someone to death mistakenly is horrible, of course. I don't think it has happened very often and I think most of the time, when it does happen, we aren't talking about squeaky clean, totally innocent people, although I'm sure someone can come up with an instance where that is exactly what did happen.

As far as whether or not we humans have the right or the wherewithal to commit someone to death, I think we as a society have to make some tough decisions about that. Do we take on that responsibility in the hope that we have a more civilized society, or does it make us less civilized?

I could go on and possibly make you even angrier with me, but I'm just saying these are the questions I was confronted with, and I think our country hasn't answered them satisfactorily yet.

The Chad Daybell case will be a death penalty case and the jurors will have to sentence him, not the judge. In death penalty cases in Idaho it is up to the jury. If the jury convicts the defendant, it goes back to the jury for sentencing. I empathize with them. This will be a heavy burden to place on them. I think it will be a bigger responsibility for them than we think, and I think that if they do sentence him to death, it will have a lasting effect on those jurors.

Even as I write this book, my mind looks to the Chad Daybell trial. I will be watching it closely, and I plan to write a sequel to this book about that trial when it is over. At the end of this book, I give you a link to my website where you can keep up on my progress and get information leading up to my publishing the sequel.

Idaho has had the death penalty since 1864 when it was still a territory, except for 1973-1976 when it was banned nationally by the Supreme Court. There have been 29 death penalty executions in Idaho since 1864 so it's pretty rare. Death by hanging was the method until 1957. It's lethal injection currently with the firing squad as a backup. The Idaho legislature has set aside $750,000 to implement the firing squad. I thought a few sandbags and a heart shaped target would do, but as we all know, the government thinks differently. There are currently 8 men and 1 woman on death row in Idaho. Idaho's last execution took place in 2012.

If you visit the now vacated Old Idaho Penitentiary, just a mile or so east of the Ada County Courthouse, you can still see the gallows that were in use until 1957. The Old Idaho Pen is made of stone quarried from the surrounding hills by inmates. There is a women's block inside the prison, and it, like the rest of the prison, is pretty bleak. Nothing but cold stone and steel. This alone could be more of a deterrent to crime than the prisons we have now. Not that the prisons we have now are all that great, but they are certainly better than what we had in the times of the Old Idaho Pen.

Do we have equal justice under the law? Is justice meted out equally in spite of one's position? Well, I will tell you the system did not seem to be broken to me here in Boise, Idaho.

Yeah, we would all like to see more of a punishment for Lori Daybell, but justice doesn't work that way. It's limited in a lot of ways for a lot of reasons, as I think it should be. Revenge is not a part of it. However, seeing justice work firsthand as I did as a juror, I have to say I was proud of what I saw.

Let's start with the prosecution. The case was circumstantial. There is almost no direct evidence Lori Daybell murdered anyone.

In fact, the only direct evidence the prosecution had positively placing her at the scene of the crime was a piece of her hair between the plastic bag and the duct tape on JJ's exhumed body. The prosecution spent a lot of time on this.

According to Keeley Coleman, the DNA analyst who testified in court, the chances of the hair belonging to anyone, but Lori Daybell were 1 in 71 billion. They had Lori Daybell's DNA on JJ's body. The only problem with that to me was Lori Daybell is his mom and a mom's hair tends to be everywhere, so they did not prove that one thing to me. In fact, I thought it would be surprising if her hair wasn't present somewhere on his body.

When I interviewed the prosecution team after the sentencing, I asked them about Lori Daybell's hair found on JJ. They said they debated whether or not to use that particular piece of evidence for just that reason. Of course, they came to the conclusion they had to use it.

How did they prove their case? How did they get a guilty verdict on all charges? Like skilled masons, they built their case stone by stone, carefully placing each piece. Simply put, they provided enough circumstantial evidence that all added up to one possible conclusion. The standard definition of circumstantial evidence is like human footsteps in the sand—you don't see the person, but you know they have been there.

Lori Daybell wasn't just aware they had been murdered. She wasn't just lying to the police to protect her brother, herself, and Chad Daybell. She had her children murdered. She caused her children to be murdered. *She* murdered her children.

But how could they prove it? How could they convince all 18 jurors beyond a reasonable doubt? It couldn't have been easy, and I wonder how many hours were spent preparing this case. It had to be a lot. When I asked them about that, they couldn't tell me because they didn't know. A lot of long days and too many hours to possibly count.

CHAPTER 5:
THE MEDIA

What role did the media play in this case? The media is the mortar that holds everything together. If the mortar rots and falls away, the whole foundation of our country is going to end up just a dusty pile of rubble.

There has been a ton of exposure since the very beginning when Kay and Larry Woodcock started asking questions. Two guys have been on this story since the beginning, Nate Eaton and Justin Lum.

Nate Eaton is a reporter for EastIdahoNews.com, a website he helped to launch in 2015. He is a four-time recipient of the prestigious Edward R. Murrow award and has been the winner of many other journalistic awards. He's covered numerous national stories including the Virginia Tech massacre and presidential candidates.

Justin Lum is a reporter from Phoenix, Arizona. He helped launch *FOX 10 Investigates: Missing in Arizona*, which is a series to shed light on missing persons cases across Arizona, especially missing people of color who, as he says, are marginalized by national media.

I was able to meet both of these reporters at the sentencing in Rexburg.

There are literally hundreds of other reporters who have covered this case, but these two have covered it from beginning to end and are still covering it. Nate Eaton was hovering over Chad Daybell's yard in a helicopter when the bodies of JJ and Tylee were found. His helicopter followed Chad Daybell's car when he fled the scene, chased by police. He was there every day of Lori Daybell's trial. Justin Lum was there for a lot of it, traveling all the way from Arizona.

But what role did they play? Media has a huge influence over the minds of the American people. We all want to know what is going on from day to day and we get our news from many different sources; TV, podcasts, YouTube, Facebook, X (formerly Twitter), etc.

I don't watch a lot of local news, but as I studied the people in the gallery, Nate Eaton's face did seem familiar to me. I had probably seen him on one of the national news networks at some point.

The news we get can set in motion a tide of sentiment that can influence an investigation. People held vigils and put together a monument of flowers and cards at Chad Daybell's property while JJ and Tylee were missing. People still believed in Chad Daybell even though he was thought by police to have a role in the case of the missing children. I guess they wanted to believe and hope for the best, and I don't think at that point, before the bodies were found or Tammy's death had been determined to be murder, anyone would have guessed the truth. It was just too gruesome and things like that just didn't happen in places like Rexburg, Idaho.

The people in the media did everything they could to help in the search for JJ and Tylee. Billboards were put up along the highway, rewards were offered for information, and it was all over the news for months, even years. Bloggers blogged and tweeters tweeted. The frustration showed in what people in the media were saying.

Nate Eaton asked Lori Daybell directly where her kids were and got no answer. You can watch him on EastIdahoNews.com describing his experience watching the trial and I think you will get a feeling for what everyone in that courtroom had to go through.

Eaton talks about Larry Woodcock sobbing as Rexburg Detective Ray Hermosillo describes his experience exhuming the bodies of JJ and Tylee. He talks about it being the first time he witnessed Lori Daybell show any emotion was when they showed us the photos of JJ and Tylee's exhumed bodies, or in Tylee's case, what was left of it. Lori Daybell appeared to be crying then. Eaton also talks about the 18 jurors who just days before had no idea they would be called into court to listen to and see "stuff that will probably never leave them."

I have more to say about that in upcoming chapters, but I will say here that Eaton was right. I could see what was coming that day as I sat in court, and we had been forewarned it would be awful. We were handed boxes of tissues and barf bags ahead of going into the courtroom.

Knowing what was coming, I prepared myself. I understood why the prosecution needed to show the pictures, but I didn't feel like I needed to see them. I told myself that I would take a quick glance at whatever it was they were going to show us and look away as quickly as possible.

Well, I did that. I bet it was milliseconds I spent actually looking at each picture. But it was too much. Those pictures are burned into my mind, and I don't think they will ever go away or even become fuzzy.

It's weird to me because I can study something for a long time and have a hard time remembering details about it, but I can see every detail of JJ's exhumed body after the shortest glance possible. After the detectives cut away all the plastic and duct tape, we could see JJ, still in his red pajamas. He had been wearing the red fire truck pajamas when we last saw him alive sitting on the couch in Lori Vallow Daybell's apartment. As I write about it, I have to look over the top of my computer where I have placed a picture of JJ and Tylee when they were still alive. They speak to me. They tell me I need to write their story. They tell me I *can* tell their story.

Dreams being dreams, I can say I haven't had one that featured the images of JJ and Tylee's exhumed bodies and I hope I never do. I have had dreams since the trial, where I felt the terror that JJ and Tylee must have felt.

There was a lot of other media in the courtroom everyday besides just Nate Eaton and Justin Lum. Some would come and go, and some were there for most of the trial. A few times I noticed people who I had to assume were probably either doing a televised newscast in front of the courthouse before the trial began for the day, or who would be after. I'm not sure if it was makeup or just the way they were dressed and how perfect their appearance was, but they looked like someone you would see on the evening news.

Others I think were bloggers. I'm not big on social media so I wouldn't have known for sure at the time. I have since gotten to know Lauren Mathias of Hidden: A True Crime Podcast, and Gigi McKelvey of Pretty Lies and Alibis. These women are legitimate investigative reporters and have a ton of knowledge about this case. When I first talked to them after the trial was over, I didn't know what I didn't know, and the information they shared with me helped me get started.

What I can say for sure is that I could hear the clacking of fingers on keyboards as the trial went along. I also heard more than one cell phone ring during court which was a big no no. Whenever that would happen, Judge Boyce would stop everything and a guard would take the phone away and set it outside the door of the courtroom. I thought that people having their phone turned on in court was really low class and reminded me of middle school behavior. I was surprised Judge Boyce put up with it at all, because it really was disruptive. A gavel may have been handy in those situations.

The media was not allowed in the courtroom at all during jury selection. There was an overflow room where they could watch the trial through a closed-circuit TV. According to News Nation, the feed was cut off whenever a juror was directly questioned. Frustrating for the media I'm sure but I think there was a lot of concern about having to sequester the jury, and I am extremely grateful that the court did everything they could to not have to do that to us. As jurors, we weren't even allowed to talk to each other about the case and I have to say a lot of the time I felt like I was back in math class trying to follow the instructor. Somehow though, just like in math class, it all came together by the end of the trial. A few times jurors would be sitting in the jury room talking about someone in the gallery or something of interest that happened but didn't really have anything to do with the case. If our guard, Steve, happened to overhear our conversation, he would remind us that we were not to talk about the case. I know he did that for our benefit and for the sake of the trial. If someone in the hall overheard and misinterpreted what we were saying, it could have caused us to be sequestered. Being sequestered is the last thing I wanted. It would have been an extreme hardship, and it was hard enough as it was. Being sequestered would mean five weeks of being totally isolated from anyone not on the jury, spending nights in a hotel, and eating takeout until we reached a verdict.

It's interesting to me watching news about the trial now that it's over. Many in the media admit how hard it was to follow. Lauren Mathias, who hosts Hidden: A True Crime Podcast, discussed how she and other journalists would talk to each other during a break and try to work through the testimony they heard. She says it was very difficult to comprehend it all and talking to each other helped them to make sense of it all.

All of the media people I mentioned above have been very generous with their time, and I couldn't have written this book without the information they have shared with me.

If you search Lori Daybell or Chad Daybell, you will find more information about the case than you could ever read or listen to. In addition, you can watch it on *Dateline NBC*, *48 Hours*, or Netflix. I'm sure there are plenty of other places to get information. I would think that for true crime enthusiasts, it would be just about the most intriguing case to learn about. In addition to being a juror, I have taken a deep dive into the case. I have learned a lot that we weren't allowed to know as jurors, but I still have a lot of unanswered questions.

CHAPTER 6:
BACK TO COURT, THE
PROSECUTION

You might think prosecuting Lori Daybell would be easy. After all, the whole world was watching this case assuming she was guilty. Everyone was angry with her for murdering her children. People watched the police make statements on TV after the children's bodies were exhumed. She had lied to the police for months saying the children were okay. So much was known about this case.

The fact remains though, the prosecution provided almost no direct evidence tying Lori Daybell to the murders. So how did they prove their case?

Fremont County prosecutor Lindsey Blake graduated from Idaho State University in 2005 and from University of Utah S.J. Quinney College of Law in 2007. She says her grandfather encouraged her to become a lawyer. She served 6 years as a public defender in Bannock County, Idaho before becoming a Fremont County prosecutor. She had been involved in two murder cases before taking on this case.

So she had some experience, but would it be enough for a case of this magnitude? I'm sure there were other prosecutors with more experience, but Lindsey Blake is not just any prosecutor. In fact, I think what best qualified her is the fact that she spent her whole life in Idaho other than a few years in Utah and Wyoming. She is a local woman. Obviously she could have gone anywhere given her qualifications and experience. She could be making a lot more money, I'm sure, if she were willing to leave Idaho, but she has chosen to stay here.

I had the opportunity to meet and interview Ms. Blake after the sentencing. She also had a few questions for me and wanted a juror's input on how her team might have done better.

They got guilty verdicts on all counts so it's hard to criticize what they presented to the jury in court. I did say that I thought they could have outlined the case for us better at the beginning, because I felt very much behind the curve most of the time. It did all come together by the end though and listening back to the transcripts of the trial, I see that they did outline the case pretty well. I just think that being so ignorant of the case, I wasn't given enough time for it to sink in.

As one of two lead prosecutors in the case, Lindsey Blake made the opening statement in court. To me she seemed immediately likable, honest, and professional. Someone who you wanted to believe. She didn't seem overly forceful or pushy, although she did strike me as a very determined person. She said this case was about "money, power and sex" and she and her team would prove beyond a reasonable doubt that Lori Daybell was guilty of two counts of murder, three counts of conspiracy to commit murder and one count of grand theft.

In his closing argument, Madison County Prosecutor Rob Wood reiterated Lindsey Blake's opening statement, saying, "Lori Vallow and Chad Daybell set in motion a chain of disturbing events that included several deaths. Along the way they included her brother Alex to participate in a conspiracy unencumbered and free of obstacles. This plan was driven by Lori Vallow's desire for, and use of money, power and sex and this plan must end today in the verdicts you render in this trial."

Early on, Blake and Wood determined they needed someone on their team with more experience in murder trials. They brought Rachael Smith onto the team. Smith is a 28-year veteran prosecutor from Missouri, having prosecuted every type of criminal case. She graduated from Washington College, and Washington School of Law in 1992. She is the founder of Smith Law and Consulting and assists prosecutors nationwide.

While Smith was the most experienced prosecuting attorney in this case, I would not have expected that from my observations of her while I was sitting on the jury. She seemed less organized than Blake or Wood. Not to say she wasn't very effective. All three prosecutors were very effective, but Smith always seemed to have more difficulty with the technology. She couldn't get the overhead projector to work when she wanted to and things like that.

In her defense, I will say I was kind of taken aback by how dysfunctional the technology was in the courtroom. One would think for such an important case, something as simple as projecting a document or picture onto a screen so the jury could see it or having a laser pointer for a witness to use with good batteries, would be worked out ahead of time. It is Idaho, however, and I would bet that other states where Smith prosecuted cases are more up to date. I might lose that bet because my sister, who is an attorney in California, the home of Silicon Valley, said, "Nope, courtroom technology is way out of date even here."

However she came off in court, when I interviewed Smith after the sentencing, I found her to be extremely focused and to the point. She definitely knew her stuff and was a confident and competent prosecutor. It seems to me that good attorneys have their own demeanor or personality in court that is singularly theirs. She had that and to me she came off as kind of a simple, down home type of person, and it worked well for her, even though I think she was anything but that.

When I asked the team if this case had affected them in their personal lives, Rob Wood's reply was, "How could it not?" Not only were their professional and personal lives overtaken by the enormity of this case, but they also had other cases going on and they couldn't just let them sit idle while they worked on this one. It seemed to me that the point was that their professional lives had overrun their personal lives, and their personal lives had suffered. And they still had the Chad Daybell case coming up. It will be mostly the same prosecution team, and Judge Boyce will be the judge. The team's most experienced prosecutor, Rachel Smith, left the prosecution team in February, 2024, just two months before the Chad Daybell trial started.

After the trial, I learned that a typical workday for the team was 16-17 hours long. They "burned a lot of midnight oil," and considered themselves night owls.

When I asked if they would hold anything back for the Chad Daybell trial, they said "it won't be the same trial."

I was curious what they looked for when selecting jurors. Was there a particular profile? They said they just wanted confident, intellectual people who would be able to follow what was presented in court. I can sure understand that because it was super hard to follow it all.

I thought their answer was interesting when I asked them how confident they were in getting guilty verdicts. They said they were confident but didn't want to take any chances because it only takes one juror to cause a mistrial.

I wasn't surprised by this. They had gone over things so thoroughly throughout the trial. At times it got monotonous, but I understood why they had to present the same argument in different ways.

During the trial, while questioning witnesses, I got the feeling the prosecution was asking them questions they knew the defense would ask in cross-examination; in other words, pre-empting the questions. I thought that was a good strategy and they admitted to doing that, and in fact, seemed pleased that I noticed. I actually felt like the prosecution took the voice away from the defense in that regard. They were that thorough in their questioning of witnesses.

So, back to how they proved their case. As we know, all the evidence except one hair found on JJ's body was circumstantial. How do you prove Lori Daybell, who wasn't proven to be at any of the murder scenes at the time of the murders, actually committed those murders? When you look at it that way, you can see why it might be hard to prove. If she wasn't even there, how could she be guilty of murder? Conspiracy to commit murder maybe, but murder?

In Idaho if you conspire to commit murder, you can be charged and convicted of murder even if you didn't actually do the stabbing, choking, shooting, or whatever it was that caused the death of your victim. What the prosecution really needed to prove was that Lori Daybell conspired to commit the murders of her children and of Tammy Daybell.

I thought, after hearing 60 witnesses called by the prosecution, Lori Daybell was certainly guilty.

Here is a summation of the facts presented to the jury:

> She lied multiple times to police.
>
> Police found items used in the murders and attempted murders in her apartment and storage unit.
>
> Her hair was found on JJ's body.
>
> Police found multiple texts and emails referring to the murders, but not explicitly.
>
> All four of the victims (I'm including Charles even though she hasn't been convicted of that one yet) were said to be *dark* by Chad and Lori Daybell and being dark meant you had to die to cast out the zombies.
>
> There was a bullet embedded in the floor beneath Charles' body.
>
> The bodies of her children were found buried in her husband's backyard. (Lori never lived in Chad's house. She was arrested in Hawaii.)
>
> The children had been bound and burned in the manner she had described as the method used to cast out zombies.

It's all circumstantial for sure. Any one of those things by itself probably would not have been enough to convict her but taken all together there is no other conclusion one could come to. So again, stone by stone, the prosecution carefully built the foundation of their case, fitting each piece together to make sure it was strong and would withstand whatever forces the defense might use to topple it.

I asked the team why they didn't seek the death penalty. After all, as of now, they are seeking death in the Chad Daybell case, and he is charged with the same crimes. The prosecution team told me the judge thought that, at some point in their preparations for this case, they didn't disclose evidence in discovery to the defense in a timely manner, so he took the death penalty off the table. Discovery just means the defense asking for and the prosecution sharing with the defense any evidence they had against the defendant . They are required to share all evidence with the defense, and they aren't supposed to hold on to it for any length of time. The prosecution isn't allowed any surprises.

I can sure see how the defense could make the argument that the prosecution didn't share evidence in a timely manner, and I can see why the judge would go along with it. Not handing over evidence immediately could have easily happened in this case. Or, at least, the defense could win an argument that it happened.

The prosecution team was working so hard and so many hours, interviewing so many witnesses and getting so much new information from them. It would have been easy for the defense to say they didn't share some of the evidence they were getting. How could you prove that argument wrong even if it were not true? So, my thought is that Judge Boyce allowed the defense to win that argument just to be as fair as he could possibly be.

I did find out later, while having a conversation about a completely different matter with a private investigator, that the defense had hired him to help get the death penalty off the table. He wouldn't tell me what that was all about or if they came up with some information that helped Judge Boyce make his decision.

When I asked the prosecution team if they thought anyone besides Lori and Chad Daybell or Alex Cox knew Tylee and JJ were dead, before their bodies were found, they said they couldn't speculate on that because of the upcoming Chad Daybell trial.

They said the same thing when I asked if they thought either Alex Cox or Joe Ryan had been murdered.

CHAPTER 7:
THE DEFENSE

I think this would be a good point in the book to take you back to what I experienced in court and give more detail about witnesses and their testimony.

What about the defense team? Were their hearts in it or did they have an impossible client?

As I said before, there were 60 witnesses for the prosecution. None for the defense. Some of the finest words I've ever heard were when Jim Archibald said, "the defense rests." This after having called not one witness. His actual words were: "Your honor, we don't believe the State has proved its case so the defense will rest."

For some reason his voice saying those words are burned into my mind. Maybe it was just such a relief to hear it after all we had to strive to understand for so long.

Most of the cross-examination by the defense was done by John Thomas, a Bonneville County public defender who was appointed by Judge Boyce. Mr. Thomas joined the defense team in April of 2022 after Lori Daybell's attorney, Mark Means, was disqualified by Judge Boyce because of a potential conflict of interest. Mr. Thomas had the appearance of someone you would trust, and experience with trying high profile cases.

In a TCU (Texas Christian University) article by Lisa Martin, she says "Like a real-life Atticus Finch, John Thomas worked ten years to free an innocent man convicted of murder and rape." He won the man's release in March 2017. According to Jordan Crane, public defender in Bonneville County, Idaho and John Thomas' boss:

"What's really amazing about this whole case is how John never gave up, even in spite of the setbacks. It didn't set well with him that an innocent man was in prison. I cannot even imagine the amount of personal time he spent working to free Chris Tapp."

That's impressive and makes Mr. Thomas someone I would definitely want defending me. I can't think of a higher compliment for an attorney than being compared to Harper Lee's character, Atticus Finch, in the book; *To Kill a Mockingbird*. My apologies to Mr. Thomas, but as an aside, I feel like I have to mention my sister here. She is an attorney and generously offered to help edit and clarify my writing of this book. She has been immensely helpful, and in fact, I think may have saved me from making some really dreadful mistakes in my explanation of the law. She'd never told me this before, but when she read this, she commented that Atticus Finch was the sole inspiration for her in becoming an attorney.

Thomas was on the swim team at TCU and was all conference in 1991. In fact, in court he mentioned being a diver in college.

I wasn't sure at the time why he brought that up. Thinking about it now, I wonder if there was some insecurity on the part of the defense team having to represent Lori Daybell. I certainly would understand that, but I felt like they were good people doing their jobs the best way they could. I have a lot of respect for those guys and the work they had to do.

Solid and sincere, Mr. Archibald and Mr. Thomas had worked together before and Mr. Thomas has prior experience in high profile cases.

Jim Archibald, the other defense attorney, has been an attorney since 1991 and has tried 85 jury trials. He had worked with Mr. Thomas before. As a public defender, Mr. Archibald was appointed to this case by Judge Boyce after Lori Daybell was declared indigent. To me, he had the look of a defense attorney. Distinctive with a graying beard that seemed to show experience, and a voice that carried well in court and was easy to listen to.

According to Nate Eaton at EastIdahoNews.com, "Jim Archibald is a seasoned attorney who has represented several high-profile clients in death penalty cases." He is one of only two death penalty certified public defenders in Idaho. He also has a private practice as a defense attorney and, interestingly, is also a family law attorney. I guess in small town Idaho you need to be a "jack of all trades." Or, maybe Mr. Archibald takes those two things very seriously and focuses on them because there is a need for him to do so.

In 2019, the ACLU filed a lawsuit against the state of Idaho claiming that public defenders are overworked and unable to adequately defend their clients. This would make money a factor in the outcome of cases where public defenders were used by their clients. If a defendant was unable to afford to hire his or her own attorney and had to use a public defender, that public defender wouldn't have the time needed to mount a proper defense. Jim

Archibald testified for the ACLU, agreeing with their argument. Since there are around 900 pending cases in Idaho, it seems like a strong argument.

Right before the sentencing, I happened to cross paths with Mr. Archibald on our way into the courtroom. He took the time to stop and shake my hand and thank me for my jury service. I thought that was very nice of him.

So it looks like even though Lori Daybell couldn't afford to hire her own defense team, and in spite of the ACLU's claim against the State of Idaho, she definitely had two very qualified public defenders on her side. I think it was a victory for the defense just to get the death penalty taken off the table.

I'm not sure what his purpose was, but when cross-examining witnesses during the trial, Mr. Thomas would spend most of his time asking mundane questions. Of course, I understand it's important to know the background of a witness to establish their credibility, but Mr. Thomas didn't really go much further than that while cross-examining most witnesses.

There was one exciting moment when Jim Archibald cross-examined prosecution witness Audrey Barattiero, Lori Daybell's former friend. Barattiero claimed that in October 2019 she had questioned Lori Daybell about where the kids were, and in response Lori Daybell threatened her, saying "she would cut me up and bury me in a place where no one would find me."

Lori Daybell called her naive and laughed at her. Lori Daybell said, "You're too naive and trusting. You're like a little child. You think the world is all unicorns and rainbows. You go around helping people and serving them. Well, I've got news for you, not everyone is a good person and not everyone can be so kind."

Audrey went on to say on the witness stand, "She said she would cut me up and was [*sic*] in the mental place to do it but would get herself in a place to do it. There would be blood and bleach and something about trash bags."

In his cross-examination, in a raised voice, Mr. Archibald asked her, "You want the jury to believe that you didn't make this last crap up?"

Finally, I thought, the defense was putting up a fight. It was short lived, but it did, however, serve to put the question in my mind: Could Audrey have been making it all up? After all, the witnesses who had been friends with Lori Vallow, or fellow preppers, were not the kind of people I would take too seriously.

When asked by Archibald why she had not brought any of this up until now, and not said anything in her testimony to the grand jury, Audrey said she had been too scared. So, apparently her testimony took the defense team by surprise. I guess Lori Daybell's powers had been neutralized enough in Audrey's mind by this point. Audrey is talking even more about what she knows now that Lori Daybell is in prison, and she now says she heard Lori Daybell say she listened to someone taking their last breath. Audrey thinks Lori Daybell was talking about Joe Ryan, who allegedly died of natural causes in 2018. Lori Daybell was not supposed to have been there when he died. Was she there? Did she murder him?

What was Lori Daybell's defense? What tactics did the defense team use to try to get a not guilty verdict in the case?

It seemed to me the defense's main point was that the prosecution wasn't sure what Lori Vallow Daybell was guilty of. Did she directly participate in the murders? Did she compel others to commit the murders? Did she advise, encourage, or command others to commit the murders? If the prosecution wasn't sure which of these were true, how could they expect the jury to convict her beyond a reasonable doubt? I think this is equivalent to a quote that I think all defense and prosecution attorneys are familiar with. It goes something like this: If the facts are on your side, argue the facts. If the facts aren't on your side, argue the law. If neither the facts nor the law are on your side, pound the table.

We listened as Rexburg Detective Ray Hermosillo spent a lot of time on the witness stand describing the exhumation of JJ and Tylee and the autopsies of their bodies in great detail. He also described items found in Lori Daybell's apartment. They found several rifles and handguns, two silencers, army knives, hazmat suits and a ghillie suit. A ghillie suit is a camouflage outfit designed to resemble whatever the background environment is. It would typically have weeds and leaves or things like that attached to it. Hunters and soldiers use it to blend into their surroundings.

We listened as Rexburg Detective Chuck Kunsaitis described how he had found a receipt for a storage unit during the search of Lori Daybell's apartment. When you're sitting in the jury box listening to witnesses, you tend to size them up. Are they believable? Are they credible witnesses? You watch their body language as they speak, make judgments on their character. Are they believable? Do they have anything to hide? Do they have something to gain by lying? Detective Kunsaitis is a huge guy; he towers over everyone. He looks extremely uncomfortable being in a courtroom in a suit and tie. My guess was he was a guy who would rather be outside somewhere. I could relate to that and sympathize with him for having to be in the spotlight. As I sat there listening to him testify, my sense was that he was very sincere and completely believable. He wouldn't do the things he had to do, like testify in court, if he wasn't. I got the opportunity to have a conversation with him at the sentencing and my impression of him was reinforced. On the witness stand in court he talked a lot about the items found in Lori Daybell's storage unit. They found bikes, a scooter, children's winter clothes, a backpack with JJ's initials, photo albums of Tylee and JJ, and other items related to the children. They also had surveillance footage of someone bringing in a spare tire and a back seat, very likely taken out of Tylee's Jeep in preparation of Alex's alleged attempted shooting of Brandon Boudreaux in Arizona, since as Detective Kunsaitis testified, the back window could not be opened without the spare tire being removed.

In his cross-examination of Detective Hermosillo, John Thomas asked him if he knew whether any of the guns and military gear were owned by Lori Daybell, and the detective's answer was no. This showed a lack of any evidence that directly tied Lori Daybell to the murders.

When asked where Lori Vallow was at the time of Tammy's murder, the answer was that Lori Vallow was in Hawaii, nowhere near Tammy. And Lori Daybell was in her apartment when JJ and Tylee were killed, not at Alex's apartment or Chad Daybell's house. We're not sure where JJ was murdered. It could have been in Lori's apartment while she was there. It could have even been in her bedroom while she was in it. JJ may have been dead when Alex carried him on his shoulders upstairs.

Were the timeline, Lori Daybell's lies, and what she had said to people like Audrey enough for the jury to convict her? Remember, she was charged with first degree murder and conspiracy to commit murder. Idaho law states she did not have to be present at the murder scenes at the time of the murders to be guilty of first-degree murder.

Remember also, according to Judge Boyce's instructions to the jury, she can be found guilty of first degree murder if the jury finds she conspired, encouraged, or compelled others to do the actual murdering.

This to me, actually made the witnesses who were associated with Lori Daybell more important than all of the detectives, FBI agents, medical examiners, etc.

In other words, the testimony of a lot of flaky prepper type people, many of whom led questionable lives, had to hold more weight than all of the forensic evidence and all of the guns, bodies, duct tape, etc. presented by extremely qualified, extremely believable professional people.

Wow, I hate to even say that but it's true. I never found myself questioning whether JJ, Tylee, Tammy, or Charles were brutally murdered. I 100% believed all of the testimony given by the law enforcement witnesses for the prosecution.

But the real question was: Did Lori Vallow Daybell do it? And none of the evidence provided by those witnesses proved that. In my mind, not even Lori Daybell's DNA between the duct tape and plastic bag found on JJ proved she was there when he was murdered.

What did prove to me she was guilty? The mountain of circumstantial evidence.

In Tammy Daybell's case, Lori Vallow Daybell was charged with conspiracy to commit murder. Tammy died on October 19, 2019. No autopsy was performed at this time as the local coroner determined she died in her sleep of natural causes. A coroner is not the same as a medical examiner. Something I had not thought of until it was explained in court. A coroner is an elected official and doesn't even need to have a law enforcement or medical background.

A medical examiner is completely different. A medical examiner is a licensed doctor and pathologist. Dr. Eric Christensen performed the autopsy on Tammy after she was exhumed on December 11, 2019, almost 2 months after she was buried.

Dr. Christensen is the Chief Medical Examiner at the Utah Department of Health and had 14 years of experience besides medical school and plenty of other training.

Testifying in court, Dr. Christensen showed us pictures of Tammy's exhumed body. It surprised me that her body looked similar to the pictures we saw from the morning she died. Dr. Christensen explained how the bruising on her arms shown in the pictures had to have happened close to the time of her death, indicating she had been held down at the time of her death. He told us about how he was able to take cross sections of the bruised tissue and estimate when the bruising occurred. If it happened after she died, she would have had no blood pressure so there would be little or no bruising. If it had happened much before her death, there would have been more healing. Honestly, it was a little hard to follow, but that was the gist of it.

We had previously seen pictures of Tammy in her bed the morning after the night she died. In those pictures we could see pink, frothy foam coming out of her mouth. The coroner thought it was caused by some kind of pneumonia or some other lung illness. This would be consistent with what Chad Daybell was telling the police, but Dr. Christensen explained it was consistent with asphyxiation.

Cammy Willmore, a Fremont County Advanced EMT and Deputy Coroner, also testified about Tammy's death. She was on call that morning and was the coroner called in to Chad and Tammy Daybell's house the morning Tammy died. She testified that Tammy's body was already cold even though Chad Daybell stated she died that morning. She also mentioned the pink, frothy foam coming out of Tammy's mouth, saying "quite a bit of foam" and "that was odd," but she said she thought it could be congestive heart failure or something similar to that.

Even though she was a Deputy Coroner as well as an Advanced EMT, she didn't have much experience with determining a cause of death, and she said she had never seen foam like that.

Willmore was not aware of the disappearance of JJ and Tylee at this point and said she had no reason at that time to suspect foul play in Tammy's death.

Remember also, this took place in the very small community of Rexburg, Idaho. Most people there are Mormon and go to the

Mormon Church, so most people there know each other, or at least know of each other. They know who the good guys are and who the bad guys are, or so they may have thought.

I did have to wonder about Chad and Tammy Daybell's son, Garth, and their other four children. Garth was there the morning of Tammy's death, and I'm told, supports his father to this day. He also seems to be suspicious of the police and prosecution. I wonder if Garth will testify in Chad Daybell's trial. I'm getting the sense that at least some of Chad and Tammy's kids will testify. It feels like John Prior is setting that up.

In his cross-examination of Lori Daybell's former best friend, Melanie Gibb, John Thomas asked her about the "castings" she and Lori Daybell participated in to remove dark spirits from the body. He asked her if the "disconnecting of cords" or "convincing the spirit to leave the body" was all done with prayer. She answered yes.

The prosecution had established that the casting of spirits from the body was Lori Daybell's justification for killing JJ and Tylee so, by asking Gibb this, the defense was trying to weaken the prosecutions' foundation.

Mr. Thomas asked Gibb if she thought it would mean people would die and she said no. My thought was, of course Gibb didn't think at that time that anyone was in danger of dying, but I think Mr. Thomas' point was this whole idea of casting, and zombies was harmless. Weird maybe, but not deadly.

Zulema Pastenes was another member of Chad and Lori Daybell's inner circle. She followed Chad and Lori Daybell and thoroughly believed in them. She even married Lori Daybell's brother Alex when Chad told her he had a vision that she was to do so. In his cross-examination of Zulema Pastenes, I think Defense Attorney John Thomas did his best to discredit her. He asked her about her spiritual beliefs. She told him and the court that she had

had visions on December 4, 2018. Prosecutor Smith objected, but Ms. Pastenes was allowed by Judge Boyce to continue.

About her visions, she said, "I remember myself in a beautiful room with a very large table with children. There was a god-like being at the head of the table."

It seemed to me that Mr. Thomas was trying to discredit her as a witness by showing that Chad Daybell's influence over her was very strong. That she must be gullible and malleable. That she, at least, was capable of believing impossible things.

Mr. Thomas also asked her about the castings, if they were done spiritually and not physically. She replied that, at the time, she thought they were done spiritually, but that she thinks now that the castings led to Tylee and JJ's deaths.

I think Mr. Thomas' point though, was that one can't just assume that someone's involvement in castings would necessarily lead to murder.

At least the defense team was trying to put some doubt into the minds of the jury. I did have misgivings about some of the witnesses called by the prosecution. I doubted their sincerity, I doubted their character, and I doubted some of what they said on the witness stand. I got the sense that some of them were more concerned with protecting themselves than they were with telling the truth. I wondered if some of them might have known more than they were admitting to knowing. I did think on the whole, they had their stories down pat. Not so much that they had colluded with each other, but that individually they had their stories well thought out. I would love to have seen some of them questioned more thoroughly, but I don't think that would have served the prosecution or the defense. The prosecution would not have wanted to show that their witness was shaky, and the defense would not have wanted to show that they knew more than what they were admitting. If that had been exposed, it would only have strengthened the prosecution's case.

As frustrating as it was, the jury had to be content with what we were allowed by both teams to hear. And that is one of the things that led me to have so many questions when the trial was over.

PART 2:
WHAT I HAVE LEARNED
SINCE THE TRIAL ENDED

CHAPTER 8:
ANSWERING QUESTIONS

After the trial was over, I walked away with more questions than answers. I knew at least some of the answers had to be out there. I would have loved to have just gotten back to what my life was prior to being called in for jury duty, but I had to get some answers. Life had changed for me, and my priorities were now different, whether I wanted them to be or not. I was filled with overwhelming emotions, and I knew I had to deal with them in some way. I felt sympathy and a desire to help the families who were hurting in ways I could not even begin to comprehend, and a sense of wanting justice for Tylee, JJ, Tammy, and Charles. I decided pretty quickly that, after getting caught up on my work, I would talk to whomever would talk to me and try to get as many of my questions answered as I could. That is really what prompted me to write this book. I felt like it would help motivate me and give me a purpose for asking the questions I desperately needed answered.

I also felt a need to tell the story of the institutions and the people within them, people whose lives had to have been changed even more profoundly than mine and my fellow jurors. I wanted to tell the story of the court system and the people who work in it—detectives, investigators, and the FBI specialists.

To my great surprise, a lot of people were willing to talk to me, I guess because I had been a juror. I didn't know it at the time, but I had the exclusive privilege of talking to the police, the prosecution, and the judge. They weren't talking to the media because the Chad Daybell trial was coming up and they had to be careful. The defense refused to talk to me, and I respect that. They had nothing to gain by talking to me. After all, I had been a juror and the jury had convicted their client of all of the charges.

I would love to have asked why they didn't have any witnesses for the defense. I would love to have asked them, if Lori Daybell was innocent, why she had lied to the police and the whole world saying her kids were okay. I would love to have asked them, if she was insane, how did she know to lie? I would have loved to have asked them, if Lori Daybell didn't kill her kids, who did? They really didn't have any answers that they could share with me. Certainly none that would benefit their client or put her in a better light.

One of the questions I am left with is how this trial has affected the defense team. I sympathize with them. I do not think they are unaffected by it. In fact, I wonder if maybe they are more affected having had the thankless job of defending Lori Daybell. Are they struggling with their role? They were given the job of defending a person who at the very least allowed her kids to be murdered and then lied about it. They must have struggled with their obligation to defend her.

Our system of justice requires them to give her the best defense they can muster, but if any case could make someone question that, it would be this one. Could they be struggling with it? I can imagine them asking themselves if they did the best they could to defend her. That was their mandate. They live by the idea that everyone is due the best defense possible, but how can anyone defend her? Lori Daybell and her two defense attorneys were alone in that courtroom. As far as I could tell, no one else in that courtroom on any given day was on their side. They did, however, make sure she got due process, which is probably the best they could do. Our system of justice doesn't focus on outcomes, it only guarantees due process of law.

The only thing that helps me come to terms with any of this is knowing and believing in the institution of our court system and the right to a defense. In a less civilized setting, it would have been impossible to defend her, which means it would have been impossible to have had justice served. Revenge maybe, but not justice. Everyone has a role and each role is equally important. The prosecution, the defense, the judge and the jury all have a responsibility to do their jobs to the best of their ability, and I would say especially the defense. I say that because the defense is in the toughest position. They're the ones who have to try to defend the indefensible and do it to the best of their ability. I think it takes great character and a huge amount of belief in the justice system to do that job and do it well.

Mr. Archibald did tell me his hands were tied because he couldn't bring up in court the fact that his client was insane, but that is all he would say. But, if she was insane, how did she know to lie? I don't think insanity explains why she did what she did. It was calculated. It might explain *how* she could do it though. She did it for money, power, and sex, but she had to be insane to be able to murder her children, so money, power, and sex were why she committed her crimes, and insanity was how she committed her crimes.

We know Judge Boyce had to put the trial off for several months waiting for Lori Daybell to be declared fit for trial by the psychiatrists watching over her. I wondered what her mental state was like during this time. Was she off-the-rails nuts, or was she just emotionally not fit for trial? I'm guessing she was just thoroughly shaken and probably not because of what she had done, but because of the fact that she was being held to account for what she had done. Lowly humans who were so far beneath her had the gall to do that to her. I haven't been able to get a firm answer to that, so I'm just speculating by what I do know about her. This is why I would love to interview her, if ever given the opportunity. I feel like in a one-on-one conversation with her, I would be able to find out where we all stand in her eyes. Am I beneath her? Does she look down on me? Does she really feel like she is an exalted being? I understand my interviewing her would give her some kind of importance I don't want to give her, and I can see why some people might think I shouldn't interview her for that reason, but I think it would be worth it just so I could write with more firsthand knowledge. I know she was put on some kind of medication. I guess it would have been something to calm her nerves. I also think Judge Boyce would have been extremely careful to make sure she was deemed fit for trial.

Other questions I had after the trial ended:

How could a mother kill her own children? What led her to the point where she was able to do it?

How could Alex have been convinced to kill Charles, Tylee, JJ and Tammy?

How did Alex really die?

How did Joe Ryan actually die?

Is anyone looking into how Joe Ryan and Alex actually died, given what we now know?

Did Melanie Gibb know the children, Tammy, or Charles had been murdered before the police caught on?

Did Zulema Pastenas know the children, Tammy, or Charles had been murdered before the police caught on?

Could Zulema have murdered Alex?

Was Melani Boudreaux involved or did she know about any of the murders or the attempted murder of her then husband Brandon? Was she following in Lori Vallow's footsteps and was it her that called for the attempted murder of Brandon?

What could possibly have made Lori Daybell think she was going to get away with it all?

Were other people on Lori Daybell's list to be murdered, and if so, who?

What would have happened if Larry and Kay had not gotten suspicious?

Why couldn't Chad and Lori Daybell have found less harmful solutions? Any number of families in Rexburg would have taken the kids in and raised them as their own.

Why weren't the police in Arizona more suspicious of Charles' death?

Does Mormonism have any fault in what happened?

Was Chad Daybell's prepper cult in any way tied to the Fundamentalist Church of Jesus Christ of Latter-Day Saints (FLDS) or could it have at least been influenced by the FLDS? Or any other offshoot of the mainstream Mormon Church? Was he influenced by Mormon fundamentalism at least?

Was Chad Daybell a Jim Jones wannabe? How could anyone be, in light of how the People's Temple ended?

I can understand why people distrust our government, but why do people live their lives on the premise that it is out to get them?

I also understand why people think they need to be prepared for some catastrophic occurrence, but why does that lead them to such extremes? Why do they think the world is about to end? Why do they think it's prophesied? Why do they read into the Bible and other teachings, some of which are extremely questionable, that the end of the world is going to happen on some particular day?

The most profound questions I had after listening to all the testimony in court were: What was Tylee's life like? Was she manipulated by her mother? Why did she seem to have her mother's back in spite of the fact that she must have known her mother was lying?

A lot of the things I experienced sitting through this trial have haunted me, but none more than Tylee. Her response to her stepfather Charles' death was bizarre to say the least. Tylee was interviewed twice by police on the day of his murder, once when she returned to Charles' house with Lori Vallow after dropping JJ at school, and again later that morning at the police station.

In the video of her standing with her mother just across the street from the house where Charles lay dead, Tylee seemed happy and seemed to enjoy being questioned by the police. There was no indication that Tylee was upset or in any kind of shock at the death of her stepfather. Later at the police station, she described the events of the morning, still showing no emotion.

Did Tylee feel safe? At what point might she have started to feel unsafe around her mother and uncle?

I think I have come to some conclusions regarding Tylee, but the conclusions I have come to don't help to make me feel any better. It just makes me more angry at her mother. Nothing, and I mean absolutely nothing excuses or justifies Lori Daybell's actions toward her daughter.

Lori Daybell's relationship with Tylee was filled with terror, manipulation, the most extreme betrayal, and finally murder, murder of the most horrific kind imaginable, murder at the hands of her mother. It fills me with rage toward Lori Daybell and I don't think that rage will ever subside. Revenge is not my place, justice is my role and we served that, but I can understand why people who loved Tylee would love to see Lori Daybell suffer. I can understand why they say anything horrible that happens to her in prison is not enough. I think seeing her in shackles during her sentencing must have felt somewhat good to some people, but I think her allocution statement probably took some of that away.

Her allocution statement felt like a slap in the face to me, and I'm sure even more so to the family of the victims in that courtroom. I wondered if that was Lori Vallow Daybell's intention. I heard gasps and could see heads shaking in disbelief as she talked about the people she had murdered. She called Tammy "my dear friend Tammy." She claimed her kids came to her and said, "You did nothing wrong here mom." She unbelievably claimed that no murders happened. "Jesus Christ knows the truth of what happened here. Jesus Christ knows that no one was murdered in this case."

I know I felt somewhat satisfied seeing her in shackles, shuffling into court, but that satisfaction was replaced once again by anger as I listened to her speak for the first time. The things she said were horrible and she said them in such a manipulative way. Was her purpose to cause hurt and anger? I put nothing past her.

CHAPTER 9:
WHY OR HOW?

People keep asking why Lori Vallow did what she did, in some attempt to make sense of it, grasping to try to understand why a mother would brutally murder her own children. It's understandable. That's what we humans do. We have the gift of thought and if we can solve a problem, we can move forward in a better way, without making the same mistakes.

There are numerous TV shows, news articles, and blogs asking why. But the "why" is easy. In the words of the prosecution, it was money, power, and sex. Lori Vallow Daybell thought she was the beneficiary of her husband's million-dollar life insurance policy and she falsely collected Social Security from his death meant for JJ, and from Joe Ryan's death meant for Tylee. That Social Security money funded her romance with Chad Daybell, and being with Chad Daybell gave her power over a lot of other people.

The real question we need to answer though is how. How can a mother kill her kids? It's happened before and it's definitely an anomaly but maybe not as rare as you might think. According to Brown University's Alpert Medical School, "filicide", the act of killing one's own child or children, happens on average 500 times per year in the United States alone. That's a bigger number than I would have ever expected.

Melissa White Towne stabbed and strangled her 5-year-old daughter Nichole in Georgia in 2022. A police affidavit described how Towne "stated she wanted to end her daughter's life because she was an evil child and did not want to deal with her anymore."

After killing her she drove her to a hospital emergency room wrapped in plastic. There are some similarities here of course. JJ was wrapped in plastic, and Lori Daybell said he was possessed or evil.

In 2018 Jennifer and Sarah Hart killed their 6 adopted children and themselves by driving off a cliff in Mendocino County California. Police found evidence of premeditation. Here again, we see a couple who are both willing to kill their children.

In 2001 Andrea Yates drowned her 5 children in a bathtub in Houston, Texas. In 2006 a jury found her not guilty by reason of insanity.

In 1995 Susan Smith was found guilty of murdering her two kids, 3-year-old Michael Daniel Smith, and 14-month-old Alexander Tyler Smith. She rolled her car into the John D. Long Lake in South Carolina with her sons strapped into their car seats.

In 1987 Marybeth Tinning was convicted of killing her 4-month-old daughter in New York State. Several other of her children had died previously under suspicious circumstances.

It happens, but how can a mother bring herself to kill her children?

Andrea Yates was insane. Okay.

Jennifer and Sarah Hart had large amounts of alcohol and Benadryl in their bloodstreams, which sort of explains that one, although a lot of people drink alcohol and take Benadryl and don't kill their children.

Melissa White Towne had previously been diagnosed with schizophrenia.

Susan Smith went on to write romantic letters to her boyfriend from her prison cell, a boyfriend who did not want children.

Marybeth Tinning was released from prison in 2018 at the age of 80 after serving 30 years. I'm surprised she survived that long in prison. People say Lori Daybell will be hated by her fellow inmates for being a child killer. I have to wonder how long she'll last. Will she die at the hands of other mothers in prison? Will she take her own life? Only time will tell.

Lori Daybell seems pretty normal. I mean if you had no idea of what she did, and if you had never seen her pictures before, you would not see anything abnormal about her. I think that's why it took a while for the police in Arizona to catch on. Not to mention, she is a master manipulator.

Listening to her talk to people was really frustrating. She said "I" way too often like everything revolves around her, and the inflection in her voice is so forceful and pushy. You must agree with her and do what she says. There is always an "or else" hidden in how she says things.

So back to the question: How does a mother kill her children? What led Lori Vallow Daybell to do the things she did? Is she insane? Is she so narcissistic she could murder her own children for her own benefit? Was she actually speaking with angels who told her that her children were possessed and needed to be killed to save their souls?

If we can answer these questions, maybe we can keep it from happening in the future. Maybe we would be able to recognize the danger signs or red flags and intercede. Unfortunately, these are questions I don't have complete answers to, but they are definitely worth thinking about.

We have to start with Lori Daybell's family and her childhood. I think it helps explain why she was so self-absorbed and narcissistic.

In August 2023, my wife and I took a road trip to Alaska to spend time with our daughter who lives up there. It's a 4,600-mile round trip, and we spent a lot of time in my pickup listening to Dr. John and Lauren Matthias' Hidden: A True Crime Podcast. Dr. Matthias is great because he is able to explain psychological theory to a layman like me in a way that I can understand. Not that I agree with everything he says, but most of it makes sense.

Dr. Matthais is a forensic psychologist and has spent a lot of time with murderers. He seems to be a pure academic, but his insights are helpful. He goes to great lengths to explain to us how Chad and Lori Daybell could kill her children.

According to Dr. Matthias, Lori Cox' father, Barry Cox, was apparently a true patriarch in the old-fashioned sense. The family was Mormon and Barry was the priesthood holder. Barry seems to have been a very narcissistic person, feeling that he was above everyone else and putting his needs and wants above everyone else's.

We also listened to Lori Cox's cousin, Megan, on Hidden: A True Crime Podcast say Barry might have been a sexual predator and he paid for Lori Cox's breast implants. Megan also says Lori Cox was the manipulator in any relationship. She could not be manipulated because she was always in charge. That is something important to know about her, especially when we consider her relationship with Chad Daybell. But why was she so manipulative? Did she learn to be to survive in a family with such a powerful father? Or did she learn it from him and follow his example?

Barry seems to have especially felt that he was above the federal government. He failed to pay his taxes and was fined for it. He even wrote a book about it called *How the American Public Can Dismantle the IRS*, and still owes hundreds of thousands of dollars in back taxes. This is important to us only because it gives us an indication of how powerfully he holds his beliefs. Fundamentalists believe the federal government is the enemy of the people and taxes are unconstitutional.

Even though the Cox family was strictly Mormon, they seem to have not followed a lot of the rules or doctrine of the Mormon church. Lori Cox's mother apparently dressed provocatively, which was a big no no in the church, and would have caused a lot of judging from the rest of the congregation.

The Cox family was also said to be more open about sex in general than what would have been considered normal, even to the point where it made people outside of the family uncomfortable.

According to Lori Cox's cousin, Megan, looks were extremely important in the Cox family. Putting on a good front and seeming to be better than everyone else was huge. She quoted Lori Cox saying, when they were young teenage girls, you had to dress a certain way if you wanted anyone to want to f— you. We could take that as somewhat normal teenage banter, but because of what we know about Lori Cox, I think we can take it to mean it was more important to her than what we would consider normal.

Megan goes on to say she thinks the deaths of Lori Cox's sisters, Lolly, who died very young, and Stacey, who was an adult when she died, were very suspicious. When Stacey died, Alex was the only one home. The rest of the family was in Hawaii. Stacey had been suffering with extreme anorexia and diabetes. The family didn't even bother to come home when Alex called to tell them Stacey was on her deathbed.

Anyway, the deeper I dig, the more strange information I come up with. Could there be more family secrets? There were a lot of deaths in Lori Daybell's life. Could murder have been part of life for Lori Cox growing up? Can we add Lolly's and Stacey's deaths to the list of suspicious deaths?

So we see that the family Lori Cox grew up in was very different and led by what we can just go ahead and call a weird father. From what I have read and listened to, I think it's safe to say he was extremely domineering, kept his family separated from most "normal" people, and held himself and his wants above all else.

The result of being raised in this way caused Lori Cox to be narcissistic herself. I have learned that, if the parents are self-absorbed and uninterested in their children, it leads to the children having to think of themselves and put themselves first. They have to fight harder than what is normal to get what they need psychologically and otherwise. When this happens in early childhood development, it can lead to the child putting himself or herself above everyone else and everyone else's needs. So the chain of narcissism is repeated, handed down from generation to generation.

What are the traits of a narcissist? Let's, for the sake of this discussion, ask what are the traits of an extreme narcissist? A total lack of empathy, extreme selfishness, a desire for power over others, being controlling, putting their personal success above everything else, a tendency to blame others for their problems, an inability to recognize their own faults, and resorting to violence when other methods don't get the desired results. Obviously Lori Daybell had no empathy for anyone. She was even willing to murder her own children to get what she wanted. That has to be the most selfish act imaginable.

Teaming up with Chad Daybell helped her to gain power over others, but even pre-Chad Daybell she seems to have insisted on it. She was the manipulator, she was in control, she was uncontrollable. She absolutely put her success above everything else, even to the point of putting herself in danger in order to get what she wanted. She married dangerous men to get away from her family, she destroyed her third husband just to get away from him, even though that meant giving up the security he provided. She must have known it was risky to murder her husband and her children and to steal their money, but she did it anyway. To this day, as I heard in her allocution statement at her sentencing, she blames others for her problems. She resorted to the most horrific type of violence to get what she wanted and seems totally incapable of taking responsibility for the position she is in. Nothing I have heard her say or have read about her gives the slightest indication she sees any fault in herself.

Historically, there have been several infamous narcissists and a lot has been written about them. People like Adolf Hitler, Ted Bundy, and O.J. Simpson have been studied intensively by psychiatrists in order to better understand narcissism. I think Lori Daybell will be added to that list.

That explains Lori Daybell's narcissism but doesn't completely explain how she could be in a frame of mind to kill her children. But now we know we have a complete and extreme narcissist, and knowing that, we can move on to other factors that led her to be who she was when she committed the murders and still seems to be today.

Having the upbringing she had and being who she was, she was open to ideas most people would not believe. She was open to the idea that she was an exalted human being. She was able to use her exalted status to, in her mind, feel she was above other people. She really believed, and I think still believes, she is infinitely smarter than everyone else.

This exalted status allowed her to believe she was a powerful being and had previous lives. In her mind, she was like Cleopatra reincarnated. Even before meeting Chad Daybell, she believed she had previous lives where she was a powerful woman. She believed she had the ability to see through the veil.

The actual Mormon (and Christian) belief is that the veil separates us from God and protects us from having knowledge we aren't yet prepared to have. The veil is God's way of revealing himself to us only when we are spiritually prepared for it.

Chad Daybell seemed to believe that when you are born, a veil is placed over you to keep you from remembering what you knew before you came again into this world. It's similar to reincarnation, but not exactly the same. The belief is we all have past lives, or what he calls probations, and people were always human in their prior lives. The more lives one has had, the more experience one would have.

In Chad and Lori Daybell's case, this led to them believing they were exalted humans in past lives. I can't explain why the idea that people have had previous lives led them to believe that their own previous lives were better than everyone else's previous lives, but we can see that they made that assumption. They don't believe they had been garbage collectors or housemaids. They believe they were walking with Jesus. I guess that's where narcissism comes in.

Okay, so exalted human beings with the ability to see through the veil. They believed they had past lives, and those lives were spent with Jesus and the angels. This meant that they had so much more knowledge than everyone else and that's why we aren't capable of understanding their actions. We simply don't know. Only they are capable of knowing.

Dr. Matthias thinks that is what Lori Daybell is saying in her phone conversation from jail with her son, Colby. She says, "You weren't there, you don't understand." It is believed that what she means by this is that Colby is incapable of understanding because she has so much more knowledge than Colby.

We get more insight on Chad Daybell from Heather Daybell, who was interviewed by Lauren Matthias and Dr John Matthias on their Hidden: A True Crime Podcast.

Heather is Chad Daybell's brother Matt's wife. Heather and Matt moved to Rexburg before Chad Daybell and his family. She says she was unhappy when Chad Daybell moved his family to Rexburg because she was afraid he would make her look bad in the church. Chad Daybell and Heather never liked each other because, according to Heather, she saw through him and knew what he was capable of. She even warned the church authorities about Chad Daybell.

Heather had been raised in a more matriarchal family where women were treated equally. She refers to Chad Daybell's father as always blaming the daughters-in-law for the problems of his sons.

She says while the kids were missing, before they were found in Chad Daybell's backyard, she talked to the bishop of her and Chad Daybell's ward, telling him she suspected Chad Daybell. The Bishop told her he was hoping for the best and seeing the best in Chad Daybell.

She felt that because of the priesthood and the fact that only men held it, her opinion didn't matter as much as Chad Daybell's, even though she held a high position in the church. She was the Relief Society President. The relief society is a women's organization in the Mormon Church. All women are members, and it is the way for women to improve themselves spiritually. She says that a man's opinion holding more weight than a woman's was true her whole life. When they were children, the girls were always blamed for the actions of the boys, and as adults, the wives were always blamed for the actions of the husbands. Whatever the reason, Chad Daybell was not excommunicated from the church until after the bodies were found.

Here we need to go back to Dr. John Matthias and his explanation for Chad Daybell. According to Dr. Matthias, it was all about mortality and controlling death for Chad Daybell. Chad Daybell was obsessed with death and his own mortality scared him, so he had to believe he was above it all.

This is very important because it is what drove him. The priesthood and the teachings of the church put him above everyone else. The priesthood, by the way, is the Mormon Church's way of saying that all men are above all women. All men have rights to the priesthood and no women do. So, men are the bosses and women are subservient. It's not to mean that the Mormon church intentionally demeans women. Women are very much valued and to be respected, but it does mean that their main role is to support the men.

In Chad Daybell's mind, he had to control death. His exalted status, his deciding who lived or died, put him in charge of mortality. I know, it's not how the rest of us think, but because of his past, it worked for him.

What about Chad Daybell's past? What was his childhood like? According to Heather, Chad Daybell's mother, Sheila, was only there to do the work and make babies. There was absolutely no respect for her, and Chad Daybell and his siblings were taught to treat her like a slave. Because of this, the children, or Chad Daybell at least, had no attachment to her. How could one be attached to such a lowly human being?

Because of this upbringing, Chad Daybell has no respect for women. Yet we hear him call Lori Vallow Daybell his "exalted goddess." Was she exalted in his eyes or was he manipulating her? Of course, he was manipulating her. He was using his position above her to get sex from her. She was way above him in the looks department, but she looked up to him because of the attention he was getting from the books he had written and because of his standing among his followers.

Why was she attracted to him? He was an overweight, middle-aged man. She used her looks and sex to manipulate him as well. She believed he was an exalted being and she wanted to be with him so she would have a higher spiritual standing as well as a higher human standing, and cult leaders always seem to have a power-seeking woman.

We're getting closer to answering the question of how they could kill their children, but there still has to be more to it. A lot of people like to say they were evil, but it's way too easy to just say they were evil. In fact, that lets everyone off the hook.

If we just say, well, they were evil, that takes all responsibility off people like Lori Daybell's father Barry or anyone else involved in their lives. It takes the responsibility off the church and their bishop. Not that any of those are in any way responsible for what happened, but that maybe our attitudes influence events or other people's actions. We all have to be willing to take responsibility for our part, if we're going to understand.

Another way to look at how Lori and Chad Daybell could kill the children is this: The power to take away the life of another person makes the killer more than human. Having the power over another human being's mortality makes a killer feel they are immortal.

In Chapter 3, I mentioned the book *Visions of Glory*. It was sitting by Lori Daybell next to the pool in Kauai when she was served the papers to produce JJ and Tylee. That book was written by John Pontius in 2017 and is astoundingly still available in the LDS bookstore. It has sold over 100,000 copies and is extremely popular among the "prepper" or "end of days" community even though it contradicts Mormon scripture. It describes the Ten Tribes and the building of the New Jerusalem, previous lives or probations, people being married to people other than who they are married to now, near death experiences, the apocalypse and all of the things that led up to what Chad and Lori Daybell became. Some people who read it take it as scripture, meaning that it is the word of God, even though the author claims it is fiction. Whatever it is or however you take it, it is extremely controversial and a lot of people, not just Chad and Lori Daybell, have used it to guide their lives and not always in a good way. I think there will be a lot more to say about it when more truth comes to light through the Chad Daybell trial and from what people are currently uncovering.

I know none of these explanations by themselves explain how Chad and Lori Daybell could do what they did, but I think that when we put it all together it makes sense in a very perverted way.

CHAPTER 10:
WHO IS CHAD DAYBELL?

Who is Chad Daybell? What is his background? What was his standing in the Mormon Church. How did he get Lori Vallow Daybell and others to believe in his BS? Why do his 5 children still believe he is innocent? Could he have been framed by Lori Vallow and her brother Alex? Was he obsessed with death?

Chad Guy Daybell was born on August 11, 1968 in Provo, Utah to parents Jack and Sheila Daybell. He grew up in Springville, Utah. Chad Daybell served as a missionary in New Jersey for the Mormon Church from July 1987 to 1989. Trent Price, a fellow missionary, called him a "Gentle Giant" and said Chad Daybell was soft spoken, but that people were drawn to him.

In August of 1985, when Chad Daybell was 17, he jumped off a cliff into the Flaming Gorge Reservoir. He talks about that leap changing the trajectory of his life. He claims to have fallen into another dimension. When he hit the water he felt a snap and thought he broke his neck. He felt a white light and could feel his spirit leaving his body.

But his spirit was snagged on something and couldn't leave. It was unable to fully detach. A new world opened around him, and he called it "the other side of the veil" and he saw "an endless white plain spreading in all directions." He said there was music, and it was warm.

Finally a friend swam out and pulled him to safety. In his book *Living on the Edge of Heaven*, he says it was his first near death experience. Near death experiences play a huge role in not only

Chad Daybell's life, but in many of the leaders of the "prepper" world. People who claimed to have had near death experiences were thought to be closer to God. Having a near death experience puts them above everyone else because they would have knowledge that others didn't have.

After his near-death experience, life went back to normal for Chad Daybell. He played high school baseball and excelled in his studies. He earned a scholarship to Brigham Young University, and graduated from there with a degree in communications.

Chad Daybell was an extremely successful missionary converting hundreds of people to the Mormon faith. The Mormon Church sends tens of thousands of young missionaries all over the world every year. I'm sure you've seen the young men in white shirts and black ties on bicycles.

Chad Daybell's mission was in New Jersey, and he doesn't have much good to say about the state. He describes seeing a lot of crime and claims to have been shot at. Apparently that didn't qualify as a near death experience. His time in New Jersey reinforced his view that Mormon country was where he wanted to spend his life. I totally get that. Whatever else you want to say about southeast Idaho and rural Utah, it is way more civilized. Less traffic, room to breathe, polite people, open land, a sense of security and safety, and just an all-around relief after spending time in a place like New jersey.

In early 1989, Chad Daybell met Tammy Douglas and the two were engaged by Thanksgiving. Their engagement photos were taken at the Springville Cemetery. That's not a place most of us would think of taking our engagement photos, but Chad was said to be consumed with death even in his younger days.

Chad Daybell's second near death experience happened in 1993 while on vacation with Tammy and his brother in La Jolla, California. He claims he was overwhelmed by the tide while swimming in the ocean. While clinging to a rock, he heard voices and saw a tunnel of light and two figures appeared. They were his Utah ancestors. They asked him if he would do two tasks and he replied yes. At that moment he came back into his body and tumbled back to shore, bloody and in need of stitches. I'm not sure what the two tasks were, but I would guess they had something to do with leading his chosen people after the second coming of Christ.

He said, "My personal veil had been opened even wider and this time it didn't close up nearly as much as it had after my Flaming Gorge experience." He believed he had a personal connection to the spirit world. He would go on to use this belief, or this claim, to influence people around him, telling them he received information that no one else was privy to.

We all have a voice in our heads, but we call it our conscience. Chad Daybell always claims that the voice in his head is some spirit, angel, Jesus, or Moroni speaking directly to him.

(According to the Mormon Church, Moroni is the angel who visited Joseph Smith and was the guardian of the golden tablets the Book of Mormon is based on. You can see a golden statue of Moroni facing the rising sun to the east on the top of any Mormon Temple.)

If nothing else, Chad is an interesting person. He authored several books with subjects ranging from prayer to the "end times." In court, Lori Daybell's attorney, Jim Archibald, called the books stupid and said Chad Daybell had weird beliefs. I confess that I haven't read most of them fully and don't feel the need to. I did start to read one but got so bored after 15 or 20 pages that I had to quit. It read like a children's story but was obviously meant for adults. I have heard others say they are poorly written and not exactly convincing. It did make me wonder though, whether Chad Daybell was that simple or was he maybe just that smart?

Was he maybe writing his books in a way that would indicate to him which people were naive and idealistic enough to follow him? In other words, if someone read his books and came to him saying they liked what they read, that would mean that person must be a sucker or a potential victim. He was also a podcaster focusing on extreme beliefs and I have the same questions about the people who followed his podcasts.

Chad Daybell did seem to have thousands of followers. He claims to have been the prophet James in a previous life or, as he called it, a previous probation.

He claimed to believe the end of the world would happen in July 2020 and the 12 tribes of Israel would survive. One of the books I tried to read was about life after July 2020. It was all about how the Mormons came together, giving over everything to the church and the church was an extremely benevolent, seemingly unendingly rich benefactor. All of a sudden things like solar power had been figured out by the Mormons and powered everything from factories to houses and somehow people were able to travel around effortlessly. He didn't explain how that worked. Maybe electric cars powered by the solar panels?

Before becoming the leader of a doomsday cult, he had been a gravedigger and cemetery sexton in good standing with the Church of Jesus Christ of Latter-Day Saints, although even then some thought that he might be too obsessed with death. He thought he should be not only the Bishop of his ward, but even the president of the whole Church of Jesus Christ of Latter-Day Saints. He really seems to have believed that he should lead the whole Mormon Church.

Through his writing and podcasts, he somehow gained a large following. Of course, one of his followers was Lori Vallow. He talked a lot about the end of times and preparing for it. He convinced his followers that he had been the prophet James in a previous life, and he had walked with Jesus. He convinced them that their path to salvation was through him. There were only 144,000 people that would survive the coming apocalypse and those would be his followers. They would be centered around Rexburg, Idaho. Why would someone want to be the leader of a bunch of people who were so naive, except to take advantage of them? Would you want to lead a bunch of people around who believed in impossible things? I wouldn't. I wouldn't want the responsibility.

He also believed, or said he believed, that people could be possessed, and that the way to save them was to kill them so that their souls could be free of whatever demonic spirit or, as he called them, zombies, had entered their bodies. He called this casting or casting out the evil spirit. There were different levels of possession and he rated people on a light or dark scale. This light or dark scale was a prominent subject in the trial because it led to all of the murders. Tammy, Charles, Tylee and JJ all were said to be dark by Chad Daybell. In fact, not only dark, but moving even lower on the dark scale.

He used this scale to manipulate people. You wouldn't want him to say you were dark. That would mean you were possessed and that would put you in danger. It appears that the more you were liked by him, the higher your number would be on the light scale. And, since he was your savior, that would be pretty important. If you did what he said you should do, you would get a higher rating from him.

This sounds eerily similar to "blood atonement." Blood atonement was a term used by some early Mormons. The idea was that the only way one could atone for one's sins was to shed his blood upon the ground as a sacrificial offering. In other words, a person would have to be killed to atone for his sins and make it to heaven.

Chad Daybell convinced Lori Vallow that they had been married in a previous life or probation, and that her name had been Elaina. They were to lead the chosen 144,000 to the promised land. This seems to be a line used by other men in the "prepper community," or at least at the Preparing a People conferences.

It seems like it wasn't very hard to convince her since she already had similar beliefs. Chad Daybell and Lori Vallow were even somehow "sealed" in the Mormon Church. Being sealed is similar to being married, but in the Mormon faith, sealing means you are joined for eternity. You will move on to the celestial kingdom together. Not sure how that happened for Chad Daybell and Lori Vallow, but it was not an official sealing accepted by the Mormon Church. Did they sneak in and do it while no one was looking? Chad Daybell was a prophet, or so he thought, so he would have had the authority to do a sealing even if it was his own and Lori Vallow's. They were actually legally married on a beach in Kauai. There are pictures of this event showing the couple dressed in white, wearing the Malachite rings Lori Vallow had ordered on Amazon, and Chad Daybell playing a ukulele. Interestingly, malachite was used to ward off evil in ancient Egypt and many cultures believed the malachite stone protected children from evil spirits. I don't believe they knew this.

It's hard to say how Chad Daybell convinced Lori Vallow of the things he convinced her of. Did she believe it, or was it a way for her to gain stature and power? He definitely had a way of twisting scripture and making his version sound believable to some. Maybe the Chad Daybell trial will shed more light.

Chad Daybell was officially excommunicated from the Mormon Church in 2020. I can't find any good explanation for that so my assumption is that the Mormon Church could no longer afford to be associated with him because of his extreme beliefs. They did not, however, excommunicate him until Tylee and JJ's bodies were found buried in his backyard. Perhaps by that time, they had simply had enough.

A lot of people believed in Chad and Lori Daybell right up until JJ and Tylee's bodies were found. The idea was that the government was once again overreaching its authority and that Lori Daybell had good reason to hide her children.

I'm told Chad Daybell's 5 children still profess his innocence. They say he was taken in by Lori Daybell and he was framed. They don't believe he would have been stupid enough to bury Tylee and JJ on his own property and that if he had, he would have dug better graves. After all, he had been a professional grave digger. But then, who would have dug the graves and how would Chad Daybell not have known about it? The property I live on is the exact same size as Chad Daybell's, and if someone dug a big hole in my yard, I would know.

One could almost go along with the argument that Chad Daybell was taken in by Lori Daybell though. He's not the smartest guy and he was definitely in awe of Lori Daybell. He called her his goddess, and looking at him, one would have to believe he felt pretty fortunate to attract any woman who could be considered good looking. The evidence is damning, however, and I think his defense will have a hard time convincing anyone he was taken by her, especially after Lori Daybell's guilty verdict.

Still, one could make an argument that Alex and Lori Vallow Daybell were actually running things and Chad Daybell was duped. It was Alex's phone that was at the graves when Tylee and JJ were buried. It was Alex who was last seen with JJ alive. It was Alex who admitted to police to killing Lori Vallow's husband Charles, and Alex's phone was known to be at the church right down the street from Tammy and Chad Daybell's house the night of her death. If only Alex could speak.

Sitting in the courtroom listening to testimony, I asked myself if there was a connection with Chad Daybell to polygamy. I was listening to see if there would be any reference to the FLDS, but that never came up.

Heather Daybell, Chad Daybell's sister-in-law, says she thinks Chad Daybell might have been a polygamist or at least a wannabe polygamist. She believes that because of his upbringing and his lack of respect for women, it was easy for him to exploit them for his own pleasure. We know a lot of his followers were women and we know most of his closest followers were women who fell for what he was saying. Did he have sexual relationships with them? I have heard people close to Chad Daybell say they suspected it, but the only way we would ever know for sure is if one of those women came forward and, so far, that hasn't happened.

CHAPTER 11:
CULTS

Chad Daybell was definitely running a cult. It may not have been as sophisticated as some of the other cults we know of, but he claimed the end of times were near and people needed to follow him in order to survive what was coming. The more I learn about cults, preppers, and the Mormon Church, the more I realize there are ties. It's all still going on in spite of what has happened with Chad Daybell. The common thread is the Mormon Church even though the Mormon Church constantly warns its parishioners against falling into these groups. It seems to be most prevalent in Southern Utah and Arizona. On the surface at least, it's all about fundamentalism, the "end times," the second coming of Christ and preparing for it all.

What it's really all about is taking advantage of gullible people, and in Chad Daybell's case, what was really happening was that Chad Daybell was victimizing vulnerable people, especially women. Where did he find these people? The Mormon Church.

It's pretty simple, really. Any intelligent person could start a cult. You just have to be smarter than your victims and willing to exploit them. Put out a premise that is ridiculous and see who falls for it. Those are your targets and your victims, your followers.

Some people say the Mormon Church is a cult. I would not say that, but I can kind of see why they say it, especially when you look into the history of the Church of Jesus Christ of Latter-Day Saints. Not the angel Moroni and the golden tablets and all of that, but the factual written history of Joseph Smith, Brigham Young and others.

Mormons are taught that their faith is more important and more true than anything an outsider, or gentile, might say. You are taught to put your questions on a shelf. In other words, put them out of your mind and trust in the church and its teachings. I'm not picking on the Mormon Church. I have a lot of good friends who are Mormon and I respect them and their faith. I do, however, have to point out the truths and the truth is that a lot of the Mormons I know who are otherwise very well educated don't have a good grasp on the actual history of the church.

On January 19, 1841, Joseph Smith declared himself to be a prophet, the first prophet of the Mormon religion. His message was that you needed to follow him in order to be saved. Joseph's wisdom was handed down straight from God. Mormons believe that true prophets can speak to God and to Angels or at least get visions from them. They believe that there can be only one living prophet. All other churches are wrong.

Of course, Joseph and his followers were persecuted. For the first 30 or so years of their existence, they were treated horribly. They built whole communities, investing their lives in their homes, businesses, and farms, and they were violently run out of the communities they had built until they finally settled in the Salt Lake Valley, where, for the most part, the church thrived under Joseph's successor Brigham Young. Brigham Young had taken over the church and become the one true prophet after Joseph Smith was murdered by a mob in Carthage, Illinois in June 1844.

Six years earlier, Missouri governor Milburn Boggs issued the "Extermination Order of 1838," ordering the murder of all Mormons living in the area. Yeah, that order actually happened and by all Mormons, he meant men, women, and children. The Mormons were stripped of any weapons they had by the non-

Mormon citizens, and they gathered at Haun's Mill for safety. When the militia showed up, the Mormon women and children fled into the woods and the men gathered in the blacksmith shop. The blacksmith shop was a log building and the logs had gaps big enough to allow the militia men to poke their rifles through. 100 rifle barrels were shoved through the logs and fired killing 17, Mormon men. Later, the wounded and three children were shot in cold blood. A militia man known as "Glaze of Caroll County" put the muzzle of his rifle to the back of a child's head and blew off the top of it. Later a militia man by the name of William Reynolds justified the brutal murder saying, "Nits will make lice." This incident was probably the worst atrocity suffered by the Mormons at the hands of the gentiles, but certainly not the only one.

There were some interesting characters and events that occurred in the early days of the settlement of the Salt Lake Valley. The Church still doesn't like to talk about the Mountain Meadows Massacre, but no longer denies that it happened.

In Wyoming, back in the days of immigration along the California trail, the trail split. Travelers could take the more northern route through Idaho with a stop at Fort Boise to re-supply, or they could veer south through the Salt Lake valley. As the Mormons settled the valley, it became a better place for wagon trains to restock. Although Brigham Young controlled the sale of supplies and kept prices high, the supplies were often desperately needed and the immigrants were willing to pay the price for them. The trail ahead would be extremely difficult through the desert and over the Sierra Nevada Mountains before dropping down into the Sacramento Valley. All of this after having survived weeks prodding their mules or oxen across the prairie where supplies dwindled and wagons and gear wore out. So many of the wagon trains chose to go to Salt Lake for restocking.

In 1857, the Baker-Fancher party, that originated in Arkansas, took the Mormon road. Their wagons needed repairs, their supplies needed restocking, and their oxen were worn out.

It was bad timing because the Mormons in Salt Lake were on edge. Brigham Young had declared martial law as President Buchanan had sent a military expedition to Salt Lake, and the Mormons were afraid they would be forced from their homes and farms once again. They had good reason to think this, given what had happened to them in the recent past, and they were determined to make their last stand in the Salt Lake Valley. They'd settled it, they'd tamed it, and they figured they had a right to it. While it was still a territory at that time, they would have to learn to live by the laws of the United States. That meant no more polygamy.

Brigham Young refused to supply the Baker-Fancher wagon train. Young's word was law in Salt Lake and he put the word out that no one was to sell supplies to the party. In spite of the fact they were a relatively rich wagon train, and desperately needed the supplies, they had no choice but to move on.

After the Baker-Fancher wagon train left Salt Lake on the way to Mountain Meadows, it was said that they had poisoned a spring, resulting in the death of Mormon cattle and people who had eaten the poisoned cattle. There is no evidence for this, and it is thought to have been an excuse for the following events.

After being refused the supplies they desperately needed, the train headed west and camped at Mountain Meadows where they thought they could rest a while and allow their stock to recover. Mountain Meadows is mostly sagebrush now, but at that time it was lush with grass and plenty of forage and good water.

My wife and I visited it a few years ago. It was a little hard to find. There aren't a lot of signs directing you there. However, once you get there, things are well marked. There is a monument built by the Mormon Church and there are signs telling what happened there.

While camped at Mountain Meadows, the Baker-Fancher party was attacked by the Nauvoo Legion, a Morman militia, and a group of Southern Paiute Indians. Both were led by Isaac C. Haight and John D Lee. The Mormons had tried to get the Paiutes to do it on their own so they could blame them later, but the Paiutes were distrusting. The Mormons disguised themselves as Paiutes and did get at least some of them to go along with the attack.

The train initially suffered some dead and wounded, but held out for 5 days. The siege ended up being successful for the Mormons though, as the wagon train was starving and dying of thirst and the wounded were suffering terribly.

Finally, after being approached by the Mormons who were carrying a white flag, the train took a deal offered by the Mormons. The Baker-Fancher party was to give up their weapons and surrender to the Mormons, who would protect them from the Paiutes, and they would not be harmed. The party must have thought the Mormons were their saviors at this point and were willing to trust them to protect them from the Paiutes, who they believed were the ones attacking them.

As they were marched out of camp, each member of the party had a Mormon by his or her side, they thought to protect them. But that was not to be. All 120 of the unarmed women, men, and older children were murdered in cold blood. The men were in the front of the line and the women could hear the gunshots after the men disappeared over a rise.

The women and children were next, and only 17 of the younger children were spared. These children were thought to be too young to be able to tell about what they had seen and were later handed off to Mormon families. Those children were eventually rescued and returned to their own families back East. Some of the children, as it turned out, were old enough to remember what had happened and talked about it later.

The bodies were also either buried in shallow graves or left exposed to the wolves and the elements. The evidence was plain to see, but it took time for the truth to be discovered mostly because the Civil War was raging back East.

John D. Lee was the supposed leader of the massacre and was later tried and executed by firing squad. Lee was the stepson of Brigham Young and is thought to have been set up by the Mormon powers that were supposed to protect the church and Brigham Young. Whether or not Brigham Young ordered the attack is still a controversial subject.

Before Lee's execution he had been banished by Brigham Young in the hope that that would put an end to the pressure put on him by President Buchannon to admit he ordered the massacre himself. He was banished to what is now called Lee's Crossing to run a ferry across the Colorado River. Lee's Crossing is now the main entrance, or "put in," for people floating the Colorado River through the Grand Canyon.

The Danites were a Mormon vigilante group formed while the Mormons were settling in Missouri in the 1830s. There is concrete evidence that they were originally sanctioned by Joseph Smith, but there is still disagreement among historians as to whether or not the group was sanctioned by the church at that time.

The official stance of the modern Mormon Church today is that the Danites existed for only 5 months and the rest is folklore. There is evidence, however, that the Danites committed ritualistic murders they called "blood atonement" through the 1850s. The question is whether or not the atrocities were sanctioned by Joseph Smith and later Brigham Young. No doubt, there is a lot of myth surrounding the Danites and a lot of folklore, but not a lot of direct evidence tying them to either man once they were "out of control." It is believed by historians that Brigham Young used Porter Rockwell, John D. Lee, and the Danites just as the mob used muscle.

Porter Rockwell is another infamous character in Mormon history. He was known as the "destroying angel," and is thought to have killed more people than Wyatt Earp, Doc Holliday, Bat

Masterson, and Tom Horn combined. He was said to have eagle-like eyesight and could kill with a rifle from a long distance, making him terrifying since his victims didn't always see him coming.

Again, the question is, were his actions sanctioned by Brigham Young, or was he a renegade? Certainly, Brigham Young and his church benefitted from some of his actions. They also, however, paid from the backlash caused by his atrocities.

Joseph Smith and his brother Hyrum were murdered by a mob in Carthage, Illinois while awaiting trial for rioting in 1844. Before settling in Salt Lake, the Mormons had already been forcibly expelled from New York, Missouri, Ohio, and Illinois. Mormon lives were ruined, houses burned, wealth lost. People starved and died from exposure. While it in no way excuses the massacre of the Baker-Fancher party at Mountain Meadows, it does explain why the Mormons might have been nervous about outsiders in their valley.

This is just some of the history of the Mormon Church. Understanding it is interesting, and I find it helpful in many ways. The early Mormons' relationship with the Native population in the Salt Lake Valley was volatile, to say the least. Brigham Young seemed to ally with them and use them when it was to the benefit of the church. He tried to manipulate them into attacking the Baker-Fancher party so he could lay the blame on them later when news got to the rest of the country—which he must have known it surely would. Of course that is not exclusive to the Mormon Church, rather it is typical of how the Native Americans were used and exploited by white people settling the West.

Some of the offshoots of the Mormon Church are what I find really interesting. These offshoots are in no way sanctioned by the Mormon Church and, in fact, are denounced by the established Church of Jesus Christ of Latter-Day Saints.

The Fundamentalist Church of Jesus Christ of Latter-Day Saints (FLDS) is probably the most well-known religious sect, or offshoot, of the Church of Jesus Christ of Latter-Day Saints. Most of its estimated 6,000 to 10,000 members live in Colorado City, Arizona and the surrounding area. People who live there simply call it Short Creek or the Crick. It's an extremely remote desert area surrounded by beautiful red cliffs, sitting right on the Arizona/Utah border. I don't think anyone lives there who is not a member of the FLDS or at least a past member who possibly has been kicked out of the church. There are apparently a lot of those exiled from the church, especially after Warren Jeffs took over the church, but they remain there because they don't understand life anywhere else. It is said that if you drive into town, you will be followed by more than one lifted pickup truck with tinted windows and you will possibly be harassed. Colorado City was way ahead of the rest of the country in terms of surveillance, having cameras placed all over town.

The FLDS is based around polygamy or living the "true" doctrine of the Mormon Church, but child abuse and "bleeding the beast" have been proven to be front and center. Bleeding the beast is just a way of normalizing stealing from the taxpayers. A man will take several wives. One will be legal, the others are, legally-speaking, single moms. As single moms, they are awarded tax dollars to help raise their children. In reality, the money they receive from the state goes into the family coffers. Of course, the percentage of single moms in the Crick is higher than anywhere else in the U.S.

Do you remember hearing about Warren Jeffs? He was all over the news back in the 2000s, and on the FBIs 10 most wanted list. This is his town and the FLDS is his church, even as he sits in jail serving a life sentence for child sexual assault. Before becoming the all-powerful prophet, he was the FLDS school principal and ruled with absolute authority. He was known to use a yardstick to spank the children until it broke. No one could question him or disagree in any way. Young boys who he had raped repeatedly had to "keep sweet"—in other words, keep their mouths shut. If they did try to tell someone about what was happening to them, they would not have been believed and they would have been severely punished by Warren Jeffs. It wasn't only his young victims who would suffer, but the victims' whole family. The property their houses were built on was owned by the church, and Jeffs was absolute leader of the church and its property so they could lose their homes, their standing in the community, and their whole family. A man could be excommunicated from the church by Warren Jeffs, his wives and children taken from him and given to another man.

While on the run and on the FBI's most wanted list, Jeffs ordered each family in his flock to do whatever they had to do to come up with and send him $1,000 per week each. This was a lot to ask as most of them had very little money and certainly none to spare. People did it though, and that funded his time on the road. He traveled in a caravan of expensive SUVs and visited places like New Orleans during Mardi Gras where he would experience life outside of the Crick.

Life inside the Crick was extremely stifling. Jeffs would dictate what people could wear, what color their clothes would be, and even the style of their hair. The women had to wear their hair in a "plygdo," and wear pastel colored prairie dresses. In a plygdo, the hair would rise high above the forehead and then come back into a braid or braids. The men had to have their sleeves to the wrist and the top button buttoned. One never knew when Jeffs would receive a revelation and their lives would be further restricted.

Jeffs made the mistake of thinking it would be a good idea to build a huge temple in Eldorado, Texas. Once he secured the land, he would order members of his flock to come live there either to construct the temple or to add to the growing community he was building. If you were called to the temple, you went, even if you were an underage girl and it meant leaving your family. He called it the YFZ Ranch. YFZ stands for Yearning For Zion. Everyone was expected to yearn for it. And everyone was expected to go if called upon or give up your daughter or wife if she were called upon, and you were expected to act like it was the biggest honor of your life.

The FBI ended up raiding the ranch and found some really disturbing things there. Behind the altar, they found a secret room with a weird white bed. They also found a vault full of information about what went on in this room. Jeffs would perform "marriages" with underage girls, some as young as 12. After the ceremony, they would be escorted into this room by Jeffs' sister wives where he would rape them. While this was happening, the sister wives kneeled on a kneeling platform attached to the bed. Some of the information they found in the vault was in the form of audiotaped recordings of these sickening crimes.

Now Jeffs communicates with his flock over the phone from jail, but they still obey everything he says, probably still ignorant or at least unbelieving of his crimes. He talks in a quiet monotone voice and sounds extremely creepy to me. Call the FLDS a church if you want, but Warren Jeffs is a cult leader and an extremely malignant narcissist.

Malignant narcissism is defined as someone who has a form of narcissism that is highly abusive. Malignant narcissists get a sense of satisfaction from hurting others and manipulate and lie to get what they want no matter how much it may hurt someone.

One can't really give Warren all the credit. Generations before him started the FLDS and conditioned it's members before he came of age and inherited it all from his father, Rulon Jeffs. I'm not sure if he took it to a new level or if the country was just ignorant of what was going on there before he came into power.

They probably just got away with it before the advent of social media and the internet.

Historically, police in the area tended to look the other way rather than have to face the challenges of confronting the problems in the Crick. Plus, the police in the Crick were "owned" by Warren Jeffs. It wasn't until the mid-2000s that authorities in Arizona and Utah were forced by public opinion to confront the lawlessness.

Father Rulon did have 60 wives and 60 children when he died in 2002 at 92 years of age. His death was a huge surprise to his flock. He was thought to be a true god who would live forever. They still think he speaks through Warren and that he will rise again someday.

You may have heard of the "lost boys" in reference to the FLDS. If young men, or teenagers really, slip up at all, they are sent away and banished from the FLDS, the only community they ever knew, and their families. The "lost boys" usually end up in the Salt Lake City area and are forced to figure out life in a world they were shielded from their whole lives. In the FLDS, if boys and young men are not willing to "fall in line, keep sweet,"—keep their mouths shut and provide cheap labor without complaining—they are just excess males. Not only not needed, but in the way of the old lecherous men who prey on the young women and girls. Their whole foundation is ripped from under them and they are literally on their own.

The FLDS and its business front, the United Effort Plan (UEP), has construction businesses and uses young men or boys for cheap labor. These are surprisingly large companies and do huge projects all over the country, including government contracted projects. They don't follow any of the labor laws which makes it easy for them to win bids on large projects. The UEP also owns all of the private land in Short Creek. People who build homes there build them on UEP land. This has led to all kinds of confusion about who actually has rights to the homes built on that land. I'm not sure if it is still this way, but when Warren Jeffs lived in Short Creek, before he was sent to prison, he would force families out of their homes, using the local police as muscle, when he expelled them from his church for whatever contrived reason he gave.

Children in Colorado City go to school at the FLDS school and are taught only what the church wants them to be taught. Traditionally young boys and girls have been sexually abused by the adults in charge of them, not just by "Uncle" Warren. A lot of times the family is aware of this abuse, but it helps with their standing in the community, so it is allowed to happen.

It's amazing to me how many of these cults based on prepping for the end of the world as we know it are run by a man who really just wants money, power, and sex. And that man will do anything to get what he wants. For some reason there seems to be a never-ending supply of people who believe the "end times" are at hand.

I thought there would be some direct connection between Chad Daybell's doomsday cult and the FLDS, but nothing that came up in court and nothing I have read since directly ties the two. Even if there is no direct connection, a lot of the fundamentalist beliefs are the same. All-powerful men and subservient women; all taxation is government theft; bleeding the beast; prophets speak directly to the dead, angels, and God; the original Mormon scripture is the only true religion. The latter means polygamy is not only okay, but you must have at least three wives to get to your celestial kingdom. The more wives and children you have, the higher your standing.

I also thought there would be evidence that Chad Daybell's doomsday cult would be more of a sex cult. After all, most cults are at their core sex cults, but I didn't hear any evidence of that. I do still wonder about that.

For more on Warren Jeffs and the FLDS you might want to read *Prophet's Prey* by Sam Brower. Another great book on Mormon fundamentalism is *Under the Banner of Heaven* by Jon Krakauer. I highly recommend both books. They are true accounts of actual events and actual people, and you couldn't come up with more dramatic, sadistic stories even if you made it all up.

There are several other splinter groups or offshoots of the Mormon Church. The Community of Christ, The Church of Jesus Christ, and The Church of Christ With the Elijah Message to name a few. A more recent one is Denver Snuffer's Remnant which is centered right here in Boise. Denver Snuffer, a lawyer, espouses that the Mormon Church lost its way a long time ago and his movement is a return to the original doctrine or covenant. The original doctrine, of course, includes polygamy, but Denver Snuffer doesn't seem to address that directly, at least not publicly.

None of these cultish churches are in any way sanctioned by the Church of Jesus Christ of Latter-Day Saints. I look at the Mormon past kind of like our country's past. Remember slavery? The burning of witches in Salem, Massachusetts? Our country's history is extremely violent. Still, we need to study the past to understand how we got to where we are now. Hiding the past or acting like it never happened doesn't help and only makes it more likely that we will repeat it.

I have to say here that the vast majority of Mormons are Mormons because they appreciate the values of the church. Family values, patriotism and love of their country; conservatism; independence and self-reliance; support of and from your neighbors, following the law of our country; and of course everything that goes with Christianity. There is a huge contrast between these Mormons, who work hard and take positions in our communities that require a big commitment, and the ones that fall into the cult category.

There are also many similar cults that have nothing to do with the Mormon Church. Do you know where the term "drink the

Kool Aid" came from? In Guyana in 1978, over 900 members of Jim Jones' People's Temple, men, women, and children, voluntarily drank a sweetened drink laced with cyanide. Actually it's even worse. The children didn't want to drink it because it tasted bad, but they were forced by their parents.

That cult believed that the American government was about to come and kill them all anyway, which absolutely was not true. At least not until Jones had his goons kill a congressman and three reporters on the airstrip in Guyana. Years of conditioning by a very powerful, convincing man had done its job.

Jim Jones also had a system of rating people, although not as clear as Chad Daybell's. It was certain, though, that if you were a young, attractive woman and were willing to have sex with Jim Jones, your standing in the community would rise.

Jonestown was based on socialist principles where each person should have been equal in spite of gender, race, etc. Black people, however, never seemed to climb the ladder. According to an article by Catherine B. Abbott and Rebecca Moore there was no black leadership and no black staff.

The People's Temple came to prominence in Redwood Valley, California, a very small community about one hundred miles north of San Francisco, connected to it by the 101 Hwy. As a young man, I lived not far from Redwood Valley, but like most people there, I had no idea about the People's Temple, what was happening there, or about Jim Jones.

Jones' minefield was the San Francisco ghetto. He and his minions were able to recruit hundreds of black laborers to work the fields in Jonestown. It must have seemed like a step up to them. An opportunity to work hard and benefit from their labors. The promise of equality for all and after all, they didn't have a lot to lose.

Jim Jones and The People's Temple had a huge following, and Jones was very influential in the 1960s and '70s. He was thought to have a close relationship with President Carter and was even thought to have his own path to the presidency. However, he rejected political life in favor of his church.

Also, Jones claimed to be a faith healer. He would "heal people" in his church for everyone to see. He claimed to pull cancerous growths out of them. He would do this right in front of hundreds of congregants. It was later shown that he used bloody chicken parts. He would have people who supposedly were crippled and couldn't walk come into the church where he would restore their ability to walk. All so obviously contrived, but his followers believed it, and even those who didn't were afraid to say so. He would have people get him information about congregants and he would claim right in front of them in church that God told him something about them and the victims believed him. In one instance, he told an elderly lady that her husband had been in an accident, but would survive his injuries. The truth was that Jim Jones had talked to her husband's doctor and gleaned this information from him.

However, Jim Jones could not have done it all on his own. His wife, Marceline, was by his side the whole way. She didn't like the fact that Jones had several mistresses but she was unwilling to give up her position in the church.

Carolyn Layton and Maria Katsaris held particularly powerful positions in the church and were thought to have played an important role in convincing the followers to commit suicide. Layton even had a child with Jim Jones.

Everyone has heard of Charles Manson and the Manson Family. When I see Lori Daybell's face now, it is as iconic and evil to me as that of Charles Manson. Charles Manson with the wild eyes and swastika on his forehead; Lori Daybell with her head turned to the side, her wavy hair covering her face.

Charles Manson was the ultimate cult leader in the 1960s. His was also a "doomsday cult," but he also used drugs like LSD to enhance his influence over his followers. He espoused an imminent apocalyptic race war between whites and blacks and was a white supremacist.

People who were around Manson at the time said he was extremely charismatic and people, especially young, malleable women, were drawn to him. He attracted large groups of followers and crowds whenever he spoke. He targeted emotionally insecure social outcasts. He used drugs and prostitution to influence them. They probably didn't know about his past. He had spent a lot of his adult life in prison, been married twice, and had a couple of kids running around who he took no responsibility for, even though they both shared his name.

A few of his followers who you may have heard of include musician Charles "Tex" Watson, porn actor Bobby Beausoleil, and Lynette "Squeaky" Fromme, who attempted to assassinate President Ford in 1975 in Sacramento, California. Other prominent people in his cult who you may have heard of are Leslie Van Houten, Susan Atkins, and Patricia Krenwinkel.

In 1969 Actress Sharon Tate, who was eight months pregnant, and four other people were ritualistically murdered in her home in the canyons above Hollywood. The following day Leno and Rosemary LaBianca were murdered. These murders were high profile and got a lot of attention. Manson's followers who committed the murders were brutal and totally unfeeling for their victims. They left messages like "Helter Skelter" and "Kill the Pigs" on the walls using the blood of their victims. They were trying to blame the murders on the Black Panthers, a militaristic group standing up for the rights of black people. Manson's idea was that the murders would get the ball rolling on the race wars he thought were coming anyway. He was also extremely ticked off at the Hollywood elite who he thought were ignoring his obvious talent as a musician. Shortly before these murders, Manson had befriended Brian Wilson of the Beach Boys. Wilson seemed to have been attracted to the free love practiced by the "family," and I'm sure some of Manson's young female followers. He even allowed the Manson family to live in his home for a while, sharing everything he had with them until it got to be too much. That seemed to be okay with Manson. He just moved on to his next victim, moving his family to the Spahn ranch where they were living when they committed the atrocious murders.

Similar to the murders committed by Lori Daybell, Manson was not present at the actual crime scenes, but was later charged and convicted of murder and conspiracy to commit murder.

Manson was still influential even while in prison until he died of colon cancer in 2017.

Have you heard of the Indian Guru, Bhagwan Shree Rajneesh and his commune in Antelope, Oregon? In the 1970s, he ran a commune and espoused free love orgies, peace, compassion, and sexual inhibition. Even after the "summer of love" in 1967, sex outside of marriage and sex for anything other than making babies was taboo in most of American culture, but with the advent of the birth control pill, people were hungry for any chance to explore their sexuality.

The commune attempted to take control of the local government through sheer numbers of voters. They recruited and bused in homeless people to fill their ranks and the ballot boxes. Antelope was an extremely conservative ranching community and this caused a battle between local ranchers and the commune. When the attempt to take over the local government failed, members of the commune attempted to poison the community by tainting the salad at a local restaurant. Dozens suffered from Salmonella poisoning.

The Bhagwan also had help. Sheela, a young Indian woman ran the commune and actually ordered the attempted poisoning of the Bhagwan's doctor. She was dedicated to the cause and had a lust for power.

It's easy to see how gullible his followers were. There is surviving footage showing them falling all over themselves when he showed up at the commune in one of his 19 gold-plated Rolls Royces. Paid for, of course, by his followers who had to hand over all of their earthly possessions and wealth to the Bhagwan. Some of his followers were successful doctors and lawyers. I'll never understand how that happens.

The supposedly peaceful commune stockpiled a massive amount of weapons and ammo, preparing to take on the U.S. government who they were sure would be coming.

The similarities between all of these cults can't be ignored: an extremely Charismatic male leader, a power-hungry woman behind him, supposed sexual freedom (usually meaning the male leader having multiple partners), socialism, doomsday imminent, and the evil U.S. government coming to get them.

All of this adds up to these cult leaders justifying all kinds of horrible behavior, just as it does for Lori and Chad Daybell. It also raises questions in my mind about why there are so many weak-minded people who are willing to give their lives over and follow these cult leaders. What are they lacking in their lives that leads them to need such questionable leadership? Is it a need to be dominated? Is it a fetish? Do they simply need someone to tell them what to do on a day-to-day basis? Is it a way to check out on the real world and its responsibilities? I really don't know.

CHAPTER 12:
WHO WAS ALEX COX?

Who was Lori Daybell's brother Alex Cox and how did he become Chad and Lori Daybell's hitman? We know he was allegedly involved in the murder of Lori Vallow Daybell's ex-husband Charles Vallow. We know he was involved in the murders of Chad Daybell's wife, Tammy, his niece Tylee, and his nephew JJ. We also know that earlier, he was involved in the attempted murders of Chad Daybell's wife, Tammy and allegedly Brandon Boudreaux, and convicted for the tasering of Joe Ryan. But how does one become a cold-blooded killer like Alex? How does an uncle so brutally murder his 16-year-old niece and 7-year-old nephew? Was Alex a serial killer?

I know this is out of chronological order but I want to talk about Alex's death first. The circumstances around his death are suspicious to me and just a little weird.

According to the medical examiner's report, he died of blood clots in his lungs and high blood pressure at the age of 51 on December 12, 2019, and his death happened to occur just one day after Tammy Daybell's body was exhumed on December 11, 2019. But why is that significant?

By the time police decided that Tammy's death was suspicious, they were starting to suspect Chad Daybell, Lori Daybell, and Alex Cox. If Alex was dead, he wouldn't be able to tell police of Chad and Lori Daybell's involvement, and Chad and Lori Daybell would be able to pin the murder on Alex.

The police report regarding Alex's death is highly redacted, but it does call the place of Alex's death a crime scene. Why? Was that procedure or did they have some reason to be suspicious? By the time of Alex's death, the police were looking for Tylee and JJ and were questioning the death of Charles Vallow and the attempted shooting of Tammy Daybell and Brandon Boudreax. So, yes, they were suspicious.

Another thing that's a little weird to me is that Alex's new wife, Zulema Pastenes, while at work, had called her son Joseph Lopez, who was at home, asking him to check on Alex. Why would she do that?

Joseph was an unemployed 25-year-old living in the basement of Zulema and Alex' house, but he hardly knew his stepfather, Alex, and had almost no contact with him prior to finding him lying on the bathroom floor, covered in his own vomit, struggling to breathe. Joseph is the one who called 911. The 911 operator tried to get Joseph to administer CPR, but he wouldn't do it.

Why would Zulema want to check on him? Did she have some reason to think he was in trouble? How could she have known something was wrong? Maybe she did know, which would certainly implicate her in his death. It's too coincidental to me to believe that Alex and Joe Ryan died of heart complications. Both had been young, healthy men. Is there some drug that is hard to trace that was used to kill them? I know police might not have had reason to be too suspicious about Joe Ryan's death, but by the time Alex died they were very suspicious. Also, once they had become suspicious, they reopened Joe Ryan's case and came to the same conclusion they had previously come to, that he died of natural causes.

Alex had also told Zulema a few days earlier that he had a money bag in the closet that was for her in the event that anything happened to him. According to Zulema's testimony on the witness stand, she thought that was weird and she questioned him about it. He just repeated that it was for her.

Zulema testified that Alex had been acting strange. He was quiet and unresponsive in the days prior to his death, which was unusual for him. He was normally very active, funny, and liked to talk and joke a lot. All of that might explain why she was concerned when he didn't answer her calls.

Also, a few days prior to Alex's death, Chad Daybell gave him a blessing over the phone. Apparently Chad Daybell passed out a lot of blessings, so I guess we can't read too much into that, but it is a little coincidental. Especially since, according to Zulema's testimony, Alex became quiet and unresponsive after that, and this is around the time when he said to Zulema, "I think I am being their fall guy." When I heard her say that from my seat in the jury box, I thought it was very telling. It kind of put things together for me. I remember thinking at the time, okay, so this is what happened. Chad and Lori Daybell had used Alex to do their dirty work. It started to make sense. He was their fall guy, and I think now, and thought at the time, that he must have had to die because of it.

It almost seems like Alex was given permission by Chad Daybell to die. In court we listened to Chad Daybell's blessing. Chad Daybell calls himself a prophet and a patriarchal member of the "Church of the Firstborn." He definitely did not have any authority from the Mormon Church to give blessings.

He said to Alex, "You had to go to great depths to achieve tremendous heights, and the fruits of those heights are beginning to be demonstrated. Now you will begin your terrestrial phase of existence. You will be a powerful servant… you will travel all over the world through portals and you will begin to gather the souls that come unto Christ."

Chad Daybell went on to call Alex a "prophet who will be looked upon as an angel on this earth." I don't know who is looking upon him as an angel. I would love to know if anyone is now or was at the time. If we could answer that question, I think we would know who else was either involved or at least aware of the murders before or when they were happening.

Alex seems to have believed in Chad Daybell to some extent. He had to have believed in him to have had him commit the horrible murders he did. But right before he died, I think Alex was questioning his beliefs and wondering if it was all true. I wonder if Alex had to die because of that.

Alex was definitely involved in Chad Daybell's *prepper* community and inner circle. He bought into the idea of the second coming of Christ and seems to have believed Chad Daybell when he told Alex that he (Chad Daybell) is *the* prophet and will lead the 144,000. We listened to Zulema on the witness stand, telling about the chilling control Chad and Lori Daybell had over Alex. Chad Daybell told Alex over and over again that Alex had prior *probations* on this earth. He tells Alex in his *patriarchal blessing* that he was a "valiant warrior, fighting for truth and righteousness and always seeking to do what is right." He tells Alex, "You have already assisted us in ways that can never be repaid. You will continue to do so as you move forward in this life. You will be known throughout this world for your good-heartedness and your ability to save souls throughout this world through portals. You will be able to gather the souls who come unto Christ. I see you as a messenger of the Lord."

This too is very telling. I think what Chad Daybell is saying to Alex is that he saved Tylee and JJ's souls by murdering them, which indicates to me that Alex did believe what Chad and Lori Daybell were telling him. It also tells me without a doubt that Alex was and always had been manipulated by his sister. He seems to finally be catching on right before he died, so he must have died understanding what he had done.

Isn't this what we want to have happen right before someone is put to death? When we sentence someone to death, we want them to come to terms with the crimes they have committed. So maybe, in some convoluted way, justice was served on Alex. Not the way we would want it to happen, of course.

Chad and Lori Daybell manipulated Alex just like Charles Manson manipulated his followers to commit brutal murder. Manson was trying to start a race war that he thought he would profit from and used drugs and propaganda to bend his followers' minds. Chad and Lori Daybell used religion, propaganda, and outright lies to manipulate Alex. They thought they would profit from the murders, gaining money, power, and sex. They convinced him that by committing those murders he was "saving souls." As we see, Alex believed it. He believed it was enough to commit murder. Right up until the day before he died. I think when Alex was faced with his own death, he began to see through all the lies and manipulation and we hear him questioning what he had done.

Still, to this day, Alex's death is listed as "natural causes." Maybe there is just so much going on in this case that the police just have to pick their battles, so to speak. I do wonder whether Zulema made a deal with the prosecutors. Will she at some point be charged in Alex's death? Did she kill Alex in self-defense, thinking he was trying to murder her?

I did ask both Detective Hermosillo and the prosecution team if there might be other charges coming for Chad and Lori Daybell, and they both said they didn't think so. Chad Daybell is charged with murder and conspiracy to commit murder in the deaths of his wife, Tammy, and Lori Daybell's children, JJ and Tylee, that's 3 counts of murder and 3 counts of conspiracy to commit murder. I also asked them if there would be other people charged in the case and they said no. I think though, that if they were investigating someone like Zulema, they might not want her to know that, so they would say no. These questions make me really glad there is a

Chad Daybell trial and that he is not able or willing to plead out. I know it would be easier for some of the living victims, but there are just too many questions still out there and I think a lot of them will be answered during his trial. I also think once his trial is over, the prosecution and police will be more able to talk about some of these things.

Alex Lamar Cox was born on January 18, 1968 in Provo, Utah to Barry and Janice Cox. He was Lori Daybell's older brother by about 4-1/2 years. At the time of his death he was 6'1" tall and weighed 210 pounds. His sister Stacey Lynne Cox Cope died at age 31 in 1998. Very few details are known about her death and later events have raised questions as to whether or not it was natural. Supposedly she suffered from extreme anorexia and liver disease. Could brother Alex or sister Lori Cox have had something to do with it? Alex was home alone with Stacey when she died. The rest of the family was in Hawaii. This seems to be a common theme; a healthy, young person dies of natural causes while people are off in Hawaii. Of course, we know Stacey wasn't healthy, but she should have been. Was she being poisoned? Who knows? We do know that Lori Daybell claims to be in contact with her through the spirit world to this day.

When Alex and Lori Cox were children, according to a friend of Lori Cox's, Alex kept trying to have sex with Lori Cox, and that would indicate that he was not normal and possibly obsessed with his sister. We don't know if he had successfully molested Lori Cox or not but given what we do know about the family and Alex and Lori Cox's relationship, I do think it's a very good possibility.

A sexual relationship between a brother and sister doesn't happen in a normal, healthy family and I think it points to the idea that Lori Cox's family might have been really messed up.

Alex's ex-wife, identified as "Debbie," did tell police that Alex had a sexual relationship with Lori Cox and they would engage in "inappropriate sexual touching" even in front of other family members. Alex would touch Lori Cox's breasts and Lori Cox would jump up on Alex and bounce around on him in a sexual manner.

"Debbie" eventually left Alex one year after marrying him in 1992, after meeting his family and seeing a strange sex dynamic and openness that scared her and made her feel uncomfortable.

Lori and Alex's father, Barry, is also said to have been very domineering and controlling to the point of being psychologically harmful to his family. According to Justin Lum, on September 3, 2022, we know Lori Vallow's son, Colby, was arrested for sexual assault of his wife. He pled guilty and was convicted. This might point to earlier family problems now negatively influencing Colby's life.

I do have to say here that I have had conversations with Alex Cox and Lori Daybell's uncle Rex and brother Adam. I think they would dispute at least some of what I have written here. In fairness, I have to say that. What I am writing is conjecture based on what other people have told me, and Rex and Adam have conversely told me that the family was really pretty normal. They were loud, outgoing, and funny, and not weird. When I brought up the subject of their family with them, they said they thought people like Debbie might be seeking their moment of fame or have some reason to exaggerate what went on in the Cox family.

Adam went on to tell me when I asked about his father Barry, that Barry was really pretty normal. He was raised to work hard in the old-fashioned sense. I think what Adam was trying to say is that Barry may have been hard in the way one might be when raised to work hard and go head on into whatever task he set his mind on. So, domineering in that sense, but not overly so. Adam told me a story of when he was set on going to a playoff football game, but Barry really wanted to go to a movie that Adam had no interest in. Adam was given no choice and had to go with the family. The movie was in a foreign language and Adam was bored to tears and resentful for missing the football game. This is just one example of Barry being hard on his kids.

Mary Tracy, Alex's good friend and fellow stand-up comedian in Phoenix, says she never would have dreamed Alex would do any harm to the kids. He was the "cool uncle."

Alex wrote to Mary while serving 90 days in prison for attacking Lori Ryan's ex-husband, Joe Ryan. She says Alex never felt any remorse for that and felt he was protecting his niece and nephew. He even tried to get Mary to gather information from Lori Ryan's mother, Janice, on Joe Ryan, so he could share it with his fellow inmates in the hope they would do harm to him. Mary also says Lori Ryan egged Alex on. She says that Lori Ryan manufactured information on Joe, and Alex believed her. This points to the idea that Lori Ryan started manipulating Alex at a young age even though Alex was almost 5 years older.

Manufacturing stories and manipulating people to do things for her definitely describes Lori Daybell. I think she learned early on how to do that, and it shows that she would tell any lies and have people do anything for her to get what she wanted.

Alex married Zulema Pastenas on November 29, 2019. Apparently the marriage was arranged by Chad Daybell. Chad Daybell had given Zulema a spiritual message saying she was to marry Alex. This was not uncommon in Chad Daybell's doomsday cult.

Strangely, Alex took Zulema's last name Pastenes. We know that is not the norm. I have no idea why he would have done that and I would love to know. Could he have been angry at his parents wanting to hurt them or distance himself from them? The only answer I can come up with is that he didn't like the Cox name.

Zulema started to feel strange about Alex not long after they were married. In an interview with Rexburg police, she describes one night with him in a motel. She and Alex went out and bought a painter's drop cloth or tarp to put on the bed. Alex had offered to give Zulema a massage, but she fell into a semi-sleep state, and Alex spent most of the time in the bathroom. She felt like she was in a fog but could still hear him talking to someone on the phone.

Zulema now believes Alex was talking to Chad and Lori Daybell and that Alex was supposed to have killed her that night. I don't know what they might have had to gain by killing her. She believes she was drugged, and that's why she was in the semi-sleep state. Apparently, at the time, she didn't think much of the incident, but it must have been terrifying for her to think about it later. It also raises a huge question to me as to whether or not drugs were used in the murders.

We know JJ had drugs in his system when he was murdered. Dr. Garth Warren, a forensic pathologist testified to that in court. There is no way to know about Tylee given the condition of her remains. I didn't hear anything about Tammy having drugs in her system when they did the autopsy on her exhumed body, other than a small amount of the medication she was taking for depression.

Could Lori Ryan have used drugs to kill Joe Ryan? Was she sophisticated enough to know how to do that and get away with it? Same question with Alex.

It would be somewhat of a relief to think that JJ and Tylee had been drugged and unable to know they were being murdered by the very people who were supposed to love, protect, and provide for them.

I have to say that I wasn't sure what to think of Zulema as she testified in court. She has a kind of strange way of speaking, and the things she was describing were pretty incredible. I wasn't aware of it at the time, but she also has contradicted her statements to the police given at different times.

Still, her testimony in court was mostly believable and she did have a lot to say. She spent several hours on the stand over two days. She would take her time answering questions, pausing for a sip of water, seeming to think over her answer. I know she had testified before the grand jury and had been interviewed repeatedly by the police. She must have been used to it by the time she testified in this trial. She must have had her answers down pat.

She certainly seems to have fallen for Chad Daybell's lies. She's definitely one of those people who seems to believe in all the spiritual hocus pocus, and that is what guides her through life.

Back to Alex. The last picture we see of Tylee alive was taken by Lori Daybell and shows Uncle Alex with Tylee and JJ in front of Old Faithful at Yellowstone National Park on September 8, 2019. Alex looks like a normal guy. He looks happy and relaxed spending time with his niece and nephew. I wonder though, if there was a purpose behind the picture and the trip to Yellowstone National Park.

Early on while everyone was searching for Tylee and JJ, people thought they may have been murdered in Yellowstone. A lot of time was spent questioning people and even searching for the bodies there.

One conclusion I can come to is that the trip was made for the purpose of taking that picture to show a normal, happy family. We know Tylee was murdered that night or early the next day, and the murder was premeditated, so it had to have had something to do with that. Could it have had something to do with drugging Tylee? Could she have been drugged on the way home? Maybe at dinner? Could she have been dead by the time they got home?

It's all conjecture, but I would sure like to know. All we know for sure is that it was Tylee's last trip anywhere and she looks happy, but she was good at making herself look happy when she was expected to. Anyway, these questions haunt me and I wish I could get the answers. I want to interview Lori Daybell and ask her in the one in a million chance that she will tell the truth for once.

So that's what we know about Alex Cox. At least as it relates to this case. He had also been a truck driver and didn't seem to be a very serious person as far as making something of himself. He was known to travel to Costa Rica where he paid women for companionship. That indicates to me that he might have been socially awkward when it came to women. It would be interesting to talk to some of the women in Costa Rica he spent time with, just to see how he was with them.

The important part is his relationship with his sister Lori Daybell, and we can see that it was weird. The whole Cox family dynamic is hard for me to understand.

CHAPTER 13:
MINING CONVERTS

It takes a mastermind to build a "successful" cult. Someone who has vision and the energy and wherewithal to make it happen. Someone who, without the flaws in his character, could run a large corporation very successfully, or might make a great politician. The ability to gain followers. A charismatic personality. Even more than that, someone who people trust implicitly.

It also, however, takes someone who is willing to exploit vulnerable people. Usually young, idealistic people who really just think things are messed up, and who have a deep desire to make things better (I know, that also describes a lot of politicians). We need young, idealistic people in our world without a doubt, but the problem can sometimes be that they don't have a good understanding, from life experience, of how the world works.

Where does one find these idealistic and gullible people? Jim Jones found them in the ghetto in San Francisco, Warren Jeffs found them in the church, Charles Manson found them in Haight Ashbury, the Bhagwan found them all over the place, Chad Daybell found them primarily in the Mormon Church.

Life as a Mormon can be very stifling, especially in a small Mormon community like Rexburg or many other small towns in Utah and Idaho. As a Mormon, one is expected to dress a certain way and behave in a certain way. Deviating from this will be noticed by your fellow Mormons, and people will talk. There is a hierarchy, and you don't get to move up unless you conform, and moving up has its advantages. Think about high school and the popular kids.

Caffeine, alcohol, tobacco, pornography, and masturbation are big no nos. However, Mormons are still humans and young adult Mormons in particular are susceptible to the temptations of the outside world. They are curious, and even in isolated and protected communities like Rexburg, they can't help but be exposed to what the rest of the world just accepts as normal. The Mormon Church provides counseling to its members who struggle with any of these things. It has become problematic for the church, though. The counselors who are sanctioned by the church and even paid by the church, put religion before what is considered best practices in terms of treatment and what is or is not considered deviant behavior.

When Chad Daybell shows up with his charismatic smile and somewhat controversial message, some people are naturally drawn in. Especially young women, it seems. To them, he seems to be more worldly and knowing than your average Mormon man. He seems to have the answers to questions they all have but can't come right out and ask. Chad may be slightly dangerous, but still accepted by the community. At least until his influence started to be too much for the church.

Mormon women tend to have their cliques or unofficial clubs. Within these cliques or clubs, they feel safe discussing things among themselves, and maybe even pushing the envelope just a little bit. Having Chad Daybell over to give a talk gave them the perfect opportunity to be a little bad without offending the church. They could ask him questions about polygamy, the end of days, or whatever and they would be safe within their clique. And Chad Daybell was more than happy to talk to them. He seems to have loved the attention and the opportunity to promote his books. According to a friend of mine who is Mormon, at least twice a year, the church warns its members not to get involved with or join these clubs or cliques.

What are the things that motivate people to join cults? Some of the answers are obvious and some are more obscure.

Some people believe that the end of the world is coming in their lifetime. Why do they believe this? Common sense says that while the end of the world must surely happen at some point, it probably won't be anytime soon. The chances of it happening during any current living person's lifetime are extremely slim.

I think the point of the New Testament is to prepare humanity for the second coming of Christ. Some individuals take that as meaning that they personally need to prepare for the end of the world. It's shortsighted for sure, but we see it over and over again. It's more likely, if you are a Christian, that you will meet your maker on your own, while the world carries on after you. Realists live their lives on that principle.

An idealist can somehow disregard what they see all around them in favor of an ideal that is appealing to them. Emotionally, it's easy to let fear of the end of the world or fear of our government guide our actions.

After all, our world, the earth, is just a tiny speck, a piece of dust in the universe. Like a bug under your feet. It certainly seems possible for something to just randomly destroy it.

And our government. Think about what happened in what is commonly known as the Waco Massacre. Another religious cult, The Branch Davidians, led by David Koresh at the Mount Carmel Center In Axtell, Texas, was put under siege by the ATF (the Bureau of Alcohol, Tobacco, Firearms, and Explosives). Bill Clinton's Attorney General Janet Reno sanctioned the raid.

Whether on purpose or by accident, the compound caught fire and many of the men, women, and children holed up inside burned to death. Was it mass suicide, was it murder perpetrated by Koresh, or was the fire caused by tear gas canisters injected into the buildings by the ATF?

The Branch Davidians were known to have a stockpile of illegal weapons, but the main reason given for the siege was the government said they had evidence of child abuse. They needed to rescue the children. Unfortunately it didn't work out that way.

The siege started on February 28, 1993 and continued until April 19, 1993. The ATF obtained a search warrant for David Koresh AKA Vernon Wayne Howell and attempted to serve it on Feb. 28. Unfortunately a local reporter tipped off a US Postal employee who happened to be Koresh's brother-in-law. By the time the ATF showed up to serve the warrant the Branch Davidians were fully armed and prepared for them. Six Branch Davidians and four ATF Agents died in the opening volley.

The ATF retreated and held the compound under siege for the next fifty-one days while both sides attempted to negotiate a way out of the stalemate. On April 19 the ATF drove tanks up to the main building and launched tear gas canisters into it. Twenty-five children and fifty-one adults died in the ensuing fire.

To this day it is unclear what started the fire that killed so many. The ATF claims it fired no live rounds into the building that day and Koresh had planned the fire. Others maybe not so trusting of the government claim live rounds *were* fired and those live rounds ignited the flammable tear gas. There is clear evidence that Koresh and his top advisor had fatal head wounds which would be inconsistent with the claim that the fire caused all of the deaths.

Whatever the cause and whatever started the standoff in the first place, the results were disastrous. And it didn't end there.

Two years later to the day, Timothy McVeigh and Terry Nichols bombed a federal building in Oklahoma City killing 168 innocent people including nineteen children. Later McVeigh stated he did it in retaliation for the government's actions at Waco.

People lost faith in our government during the Vietnam war and the protests in the 1960s. In the Kent State Massacre, four college students protesting the war were killed by the Ohio National Guard and several others were wounded when the National Guard opened fire. Hundreds of thousands of young Americans died in the somewhat questionable war in Vietnam.

It's easy to see why people don't trust the government. We're not supposed to trust our government. We are supposed to question our government and hold those in power accountable. That's how our system of government is set up. But does our system of government breed exploitable people? We do seem to have a never-ending supply of them. These cults keep happening.

Chad Daybell found his followers mainly in the Mormon Church although he did have others who weren't Mormon.

So, converts are easy to find. I said before that it merely takes someone willing to exploit vulnerable people and then it's simple. You set up a premise: the end of the world, government overreach, free love, or whatever. You tell people that you are the only one who can save them or provide that for them. You see who falls for it.

Chad wrote books, had podcasts, and would speak at prepper conventions. Prepper conventions are an industry of their own. Promoting self-reliance and survivability in the event of natural disaster, war, disruption of supply chain, etc. At these conventions, people could buy items they would need to survive, buy books giving information on how to survive, and meet people who they might need to coordinate with when the end time came. Since the whole Covid-19 pandemic and the associated problems, prepping has become even more popular. Covid-19, and the government's reaction to it reinforces the idea that something could go terribly wrong, to the point where people will need to be prepared and independently able to fend for themselves.

And fending for themselves includes being able to defend themselves. The idea is that no one will have what they need to survive so everyone will turn into thieves. Since you, as a prepper, have prepared, you will need to be able to defend yourself and your family against those who were less insightful or less prepared. In other words, you better have a semi-automatic rifle or two and know how to use it. Oh, and plenty of ammunition.

I'm not making light of this idea. After all, the Second Amendment to the U.S. Constitution says, as citizens of the United States, we have the right to: "A well-regulated Militia being necessary to the security of a free State, the right of the people to keep and bear Arms shall not be infringed."

This amendment is not only meant to allow for citizens to protect themselves from each other or from foreign invaders, but also from our own government. Our forefathers meant for it to be a way of keeping our government in check. Some now say that argument has become ridiculous. After all, our government now has weapons so powerful they could end the world. Hmmm, again reinforcing the preppers' needs to be prepared!

In light of all the mass shootings and gun violence happening in our country, this right to bear arms has become extremely controversial. Of course, the idea that the government could take away that right only serves to further encourage preppers.

And, in a truly free state like Idaho which adheres to the constitutional right of its citizens to carry firearms, good people get to carry guns too. It's not just the criminals walking around with a gun hidden away. I firmly believe that that simple fact, the fact that if you break into someone's home, that someone is more than likely going to be armed and ready to defend himself or herself and his or her family and property, discourages criminals from committing crimes. Also, if you do commit that crime in Idaho, you are more likely to be punished for it. Much easier to commit that crime in a state that is more friendly to it.

In fact, I would go so far as to say it is the responsibility of all good people who are capable, to be the defenders of not only your own property and family, but also your neighbor who may not be in a position to defend himself or herself. Here's an example of what I mean by defending your neighbor: In 2022 twenty-year-old Jonathan Sapirman opened fire in an Indiana shopping mall food court. He killed three totally innocent, unexpecting people and wounded two more before a gun-carrying citizen named Elisjsha Dicken stopped him by shooting him eight times with his own gun. How many lives did he save? It's impossible to know, but it could have been many. It's a clear-cut example of a bad guy with a gun being neutralized by a good guy with a gun.

So, as gun loving Americans with the Wild West in our hearts, good luck taking away our guns. Not that they won't keep trying.

Back to Chad Daybell. Chad Daybell had managed to create a following of thousands based mainly on his prepper ideas, but his inner circle was small. Typical of a cult leader. To manage a cult you need others who are willing to go along with you to the point where they are aware of the exploitation and willing to participate for a reason. That reason is the power they acquire within the cult, always given or taken away by the all-powerful leader. Remember the light or dark scale? It was pretty easy to get on the dark scale and very hard to move up on the light scale. And who had the voice of God in his head and the ability to move one up or down on the scale? Chad Daybell and only Chad Daybell.

And could Lori Vallow Daybell have been on some level a victim of Chad Daybell or was this the perfect union of two people with the same vision?

Lori Vallow also believed she spoke with God or at least that God spoke directly to her. In fact, way back in 2004 she was a contestant on "Wheel of Fortune," at least 14 years before meeting Chad Daybell. She talked then of hearing the voice of God telling her to go on the show. She won more than $17,000 so I guess it worked out for her. It didn't work out as well for her earlier that same year when she participated in the Mrs. Texas beauty pageant. She fell short and was dropped from the pageant in the early stages.

I believe that Lori Vallow Daybell, Chad Daybell, and some of their followers were in on the scheme, willing to take advantage of people, take their money and even their lives if necessary. Why? In order to promote their own lives, whether monetarily, for the sake of sex, or for the sake of power. Power moved you up on the light/dark scale and moving up on the light/dark scale gave you power.

Listening to some of the witnesses left me wondering if they had been duped by Chad and Lori Daybell or if they were in on the hoax like Lori Daybell.

Could some of Chad and Lori Daybell's followers have known JJ and Tylee were in danger? Could some of them have known Tammy and Brandon were in danger? Could they at least have had some information that might have helped the police solve the mystery of the disappearance of JJ and Tylee sooner? Some of the witnesses who testified seemed extremely shaky. Not that they were actually shaking on the stand. More like they didn't seem sincere. They didn't seem like the kind of people whose story I could trust. Were they covering their butts or were they truly ignorant of what was actually happening?

The only truly believable witnesses who had been associated with Lori Daybell were her sister, Summer Shiflet, her son Colby Ryan and her ex-sister-in-law Kay Woodcock. Of course, none of them were involved with Chad Daybell or his cult.

Lori Daybell's niece, Melani Boudreaux (now Pawlowski), seemed to want her ex-husband Brandon dead, and there is evidence that she was close with Lori Daybell and part of their doomsday cult.

Melani claimed it was not a cult and stuck up for Lori Daybell. In November, 2019 she was arrested at the home of ex-husband

Brandon Boudreaux and convicted of criminal trespass. Her father-in-law was in the house at the time and feared for his life as Melani beat on the door between the house and garage. He was aware of some of the crimes already committed by the cult and that they had said certain people were zombies and needed to die, so he called the police. Alex Cox was with her at the time, but he was outside sitting in his truck when police arrived.

I have a hard time believing that some of the witnesses hadn't known something that at least could have helped the police figure things out and possibly could have kept events from unfolding the way they did.

Melanie Gibb, a close friend of Lori Daybell (don't confuse her with Melani Boudreaux) since the two met in 2018, testified in court and her testimony was pretty damning for Lori Daybell.

Melanie Gibb said Lori Daybell had changed after she met Chad Daybell. Melanie didn't go along with the things Lori Daybell was saying about zombies and the idea that JJ was possessed. She didn't go along with Lori Daybell's idea that she and Chad Daybell had been married in a previous life.

She became suspicious and actually recorded a phone call between her and Lori Daybell on December 8, 2019, and that phone call was played in court.

In the phone call, Lori Daybell says the kids are okay but won't tell Melanie where they are. "Where is he? I've been asking where is he?" Gibb said on the phone call, referring to JJ.

Lori Daybell answered: "I could tell everything—where JJ is right now and that would not be good for JJ." Lori also said JJ was possessed by an evil spirit and would crawl up on top of the refrigerator and cabinets. She said he knocked over and broke a picture of Christ.

We know JJ had autism but crawling up on the refrigerator and cabinets still sounds a little extreme. It seemed that Lori

Daybell was trying to justify something. In the phone call, Lori Daybell keeps reiterating that JJ is safe but people are after him. When Gibb keeps questioning, Lori and Chad Daybell just tell her they aren't saying where JJ is in order to keep Gibb safe. Gibb asks why she would be in danger and who would be after JJ, but she just keeps getting vague answers. Still, we clearly hear both Chad and Lori Daybell lie to her.

When Lori Daybell's attorney, John Thomas, cross-examined Melanie, we found out that Melanie had taken part in some of the "casting out of devils and evil spirits." Melanie explained that she thought it was innocent.

Melanie Gibb seemed to me to be a person who was initially taken in by Chad and Lori Daybell. She may have been a little charmed by them, but eventually realized they might be a little too far out there for her. Still, she was a very close friend to Lori Daybell, and I think she was shocked and offended when Lori Daybell wouldn't tell her where the kids were, even before she knew they had been murdered and buried in Chad Daybell's backyard.

Melanie Gibb is definitely one of the people I wonder about. Did she know about at least some of Lori and Chad Daybell's crimes? Was she involved in any of them? Is she covering for herself? We at least know that at some point she decided to cooperate with the police, but was that in order for her to keep herself out of trouble? Maybe we'll never know.

Some of the most chilling testimony I thought came from Zulema Pastenes, a close friend of Lori Daybell, who as I said earlier, eventually married Lori Daybell's brother Alex in Las Vegas in November 2019. She seemed to hold nothing back on the witness stand, and besides the police, seemed to be one of the few witnesses who believed Lori Daybell was guilty and wasn't taken in by her. Of course, she was taken in by Lori Daybell originally, and she was definitely a "convert," but by the time she took the witness stand, she was clearly fully aware of what Lori Daybell had done to her kids.

Zulema's testimony started with Alex's shooting of Lori Daybell's ex-husband, Charles Vallow: "I asked him [Alex] if he was okay after he had just shot someone, I thought he would be like in shock or struggling with what had happened and he said, 'Zulema, he was a zombie.'"

Zulema testified that Alex believed everything Lori Daybell told him. It's hard to swallow, but if this is true it's really sad.

She said Lori Daybell was convincing and vivacious and had a very high spiritual standing.

Lori Daybell told her she had been visited by Jesus and had visitations by angels including Moroni.

The most damning testimony came when Zulema described Lori Daybell's explanation about how possessed people were to be dealt with. "Dispel, burn, cast out and get rid of them." Also "binding." Tylee had been burned and JJ was bound with duct tape.

Zulema went on to say that Chad Daybell claimed he had been Heavenly Father, Jesus, and the Holy Ghost and he and Lori Daybell had been 7 times on this earth.

On the witness stand Zulema said they made it all up, but my feeling is that she believed it all at the time. She said she originally thought they were kind, loving, law abiding, and righteous.

She went on to say she had gone with Lori Vallow to Preparing a People conferences. She said when Lori Vallow met Chad Daybell, she immediately started "flirting and putting the moves on him."

Lori Vallow told Zulema that ex-husband Charles was possessed by a dark spirit or demon named Garrett and she could see that Charles had gotten shorter. Apparently his being shorter was supposed to support the argument that he was possessed.

Zulema attended multiple "castings" to cast out the evil spirit, Garrett. She said it was a group of girlfriends holding hands in a circle and it seemed pretty innocent. But, after that, according to Lori Vallow, Charles was taken over by Ned Snyder, an even more powerful evil spirit. Apparently there is a window of a few minutes when, after a casting, a new spirit can enter one's body.

As we saw earlier, Alex had told Zulema at one point that he thought he was "being their fall guy," so he must have had some understanding of what he had done. "I think I am being their fall guy, either I am a man of God, or I am not," is what he said.

Lori Vallow told Zulema that Tammy had passed away because they were finally able to do a casting of a demon.

Lori Vallow also told Zulema that Rexburg was going to be a place where there would be soldiers and warriors that would be defending that area and the area had been prepared by the church. "I think they were lying to me," Zulema unbelievably said on the witness stand, indicating she might still have some question.

What do we make of Zulema Pastenas? Extremely gullible for sure. Looking for answers where there are no answers, at least not any that we are meant to find. Idealistic to an extreme degree. But does that make her a criminal? Did she know what Chad and Lori Daybell were up to early enough to have stopped events from unfolding the way they did? I don't know.

Back to the question, how does one find converts? As I said earlier, Chad Daybell found them primarily in the Mormon Church. But why would the Mormon Church be a good place to find people willing to go along with his premise? His premise was that the world was coming to an end on July 22, 2020. He was in direct contact with God, and he would lead his chosen people to the promised land.

The Mormon Church does espouse that the prophet or prophets do have a direct connection to God and get visions and messages directly from God. The idea of prophets in the Mormon Church is a little unclear to me. The president of the church is a prophet. There have been 17 presidents since the origination of the Mormon Church, starting, of course, with Joseph Smith in 1830. Can someone other than the president be a prophet? Technically, I would say no, but there have been many who have claimed they are prophets. If Chad Daybell can convince some people he is a prophet, it's not a huge stretch to believe he's getting messages from God. And, if he is getting messages directly from God, one had better listen.

I'll admit, it's a stretch, but actually that's the point. Again, if you find people gullible enough to believe your lies, you have at least the beginning of a cult. You start with people who go along with your premise, and you keep adding on with half-truths that sound somewhat believable. Play to their fears and insecurities. Convince them that danger is coming from somewhere and then convince them to follow you. You have the answers they are looking for. As you gain true believers, move them into positions of power and allow them to benefit from that power. They will back up your lies, furthering other's belief in you.

Even so, that will never explain how a mother, her brother, and a stepfather murder their children. Lori Daybell and Alex Cox had to have truly believed what Lori and Chad Daybell were espousing. The world was coming to an end, the children's bodies were invaded by zombies and were already dead, and the only way their souls could be released and sent to heaven would be to cast out the zombies by killing the bodies.

But that contradicts the prosecution's argument that it was all about money, power, and sex. So was it money, power, and sex, or was it the end of the world? Well, the end of the world didn't happen. At least not when Chad Daybell said it would. July 22, 2020 has come and gone. So I guess we'll go with money, power, and sex. Either way, Lori Daybell needs to spend the rest of her life in prison. Hopefully someday the truth will come to her and that would be better justice to me than the death penalty.

CHAPTER 14:
DID SEX COME INTO PLAY?

We know that Chad Daybell and Lori Vallow Daybell had a sexual relationship. In fact, Chad Daybell told Lori Vallow that they had been married in a previous life the first time they met at a Preparing a People conference in St. George, Utah in 2018. I would love to know if that was a line he used on other women. I have heard it was a common line used by the men in the inner circle of the Preparing a People conferences.

Later Chad called himself an adult Harry Potter living with the Dudleys, referring I guess to having to live with his wife, Tammy, when he would rather be with Lori Vallow. He talked to Lori Vallow about their previous lives as James and Elaina and apparently wrote about that in one of his novels. I haven't read it, but I've been told it is a somewhat erotic novel.

Lori Vallow said she could have Chad Daybell come to her spiritually at night. She even had a portal in her closet that he would come through. Bizarre, I know, but that is her claim. He also called her his "exalted goddess." The terms "loin fire" and "storm in my pants" came into play at some point.

FBI Agent Douglas Hart had to read several texts between Chad Daybell and Lori Vallow aloud in court. Here is some of the text:

Chad: "I need so badly to just gently kiss you… for hours."
Chad: "It would likely lead to other activities."
Lori: "Likely or luckily?"
Chad: "It would lead to nakedness."

Okay, we all have texts we wouldn't like to have read out loud in front of a bunch of people, but remember, Chad Daybell and Lori Vallow were still married to their living spouses, Tammy and Charles, at that time.

Lori Daybell's cellmate, after Lori Daybell was extradited from Hawaii back to Idaho, talked about her conversations with Lori Daybell regarding Chad Daybell. She said Lori Daybell's comments were nauseating. She also said Lori Daybell's phone conversations with Chad Daybell, which she couldn't help overhear, were nauseating.

But what about all the other women in Chad's life? Or men for that matter? According to *Inside Edition*, in 2018 Julie Rowe was sexually assaulted by Chad Daybell and that was part of a pattern of inappropriate and sometimes "predatory" behavior toward women.

Julie Rowe is an author and published books with Chad Daybell between 2014 and 2017. She also claimed to have had a near death experience. She says Chad Daybell forcibly kissed her, got on top of her and, while they were clothed, rubbed his genitals against her body.

Eric Smith, an Idaho based author, who at one time was Chad Daybell's friend, believes Chad Daybell used his spiritual knowledge and gifts to lure women in. According to *Edition Digital,* Chad Daybell used "this ability he had to present himself as a real pious person with humility-like a guru."

"Chad was using this doctrine to groom women, to get them to do something that normally they wouldn't do", Smith said. "Or in other words, give up their creative power to him, for his own gain. He was no longer following the creator's plan of agency, but he was trying to get women to do things that would give him more power."

In the Mormon faith, "agency" is the ability and privilege God gives us to choose and act for ourselves.

Smith went on to say he attended meetings with Chad Daybell at people's homes. It would usually be a small group of women. According to *Inside Edition,* Smith said he had been to several small events in the Rexburg area with Chad Daybell, and at one the women wanted to talk about polygamy. Smith said they were interested in fringe ideas that were inappropriate and divisive for families.

There was a night in 2018 at a *Preparing a People* Conference in Mesa, Arizona when Lori Vallow invited Chad Daybell, Melanie Gibb, someone named Lisa, and a few others to spend the night at her house. Lori Vallow's husband and children were out of town at the time.

Still, none of the testimony at the trial broached the subject of sex, and I don't know if that was by design or if none of the witnesses were willing to talk about that aspect of their relationship with Chad Daybell. It could be that the prosecution might have had trouble getting some of the witnesses to testify about those details.

For sure, Chad Daybell had plenty of opportunities with several women. According to Detective Hermosillo's testimony in court, Chad Daybell did lie about knowing Lori Vallow (now Daybell) to the police in Rexburg when they first questioned him outside of Lori Daybell's apartment. This was after they became concerned about the whereabouts of Tylee and JJ. He acted like he barely knew who she was in spite of the fact that they had just married. Could that be an indication that Chad Daybell was used to lying about his relationships with women?

There have been questions about whether Chad Daybell was trying to get Tammy to agree to allow him to enter into a polygamist lifestyle. One thought is that she didn't go along with it and that is why he had to kill her.

Why are some women attracted to a man like Chad Daybell? Do they see him as a powerful person and are they attracted to that?

According to Clinical Psychologist Dr. Marianne Brandon, "Women are evolutionarily designed to desire men in powerful positions. That's because, from an evolutionary perspective, power means that a man can offer a safe, secure home life for her, and have the resources to better meet their children's needs. Thus, offspring have a better chance of surviving and thriving into adulthood, and ultimately continue to pass their DNA onto the next generation."

In addition, women are also socially conditioned for this, particularly in a male-dominated patriarchal society such as Mormonism.

Okay, I know that is over-generalizing and certainly doesn't describe all women, but it does help to explain why some women are attracted to men who they see as being in a position of power. Also, some men are more than willing to exploit vulnerable women. Especially cult leaders.

I have read enough about the *prepper* conventions to have this question: Could the conventions have been a way for Mormon men and women to allow themselves to explore sex with partners who were not their spouses, and to excuse themselves for it because they were part of something that was bigger than or above the teachings of the Mormon Church? And, if this is true, was sex used as a way to manipulate people like a carrot for a rabbit?

I have heard that other men in the prepper community, besides Chad Daybell, used the line on women that they had been married in a previous life, so whatever they did was okay, and, in fact, it was good and proper. Was that the line that gave permission? I think so, at least in Chad Daybell's inner circle. I think they were using the prepper conventions like a sex party or at least an opportunity to "hook up." I think in the inner circle, it was known that after the convention the real party would start. I think that when Lori Vallow showed up at one, Chad Daybell used his common line on her and as we have seen, she fell for it hook, line, and sinker.

All of this goes really deep and it's still going on even though "Preparing a People" no longer exists. There is a whole cult or cult-like genre of book writers, podcasters, and all-around prepper leaders who hold conventions with an underlying theme: I am a powerful prophet, I have knowledge that others don't have. You can come into the fold and be free of all of the conventions that stifle you because, with me, you are an exalted being above all of the rules that hold you back. With me you are free and safe to explore because *I* give you permission. Even if people don't actually believe any of this, they can give themselves permission using the excuse that they do believe it.

I don't have any other indication that Chad Daybell was some kind of sex guru. I keep hearing how unattractive he is as if that matters, but are any of the really successful sex cult leaders we know of attractive? I really thought there might be some ties to the FLDS and possibly some pedophilia happening. Some real Ghislane Maxwell/Jeffrey Epstein type stuff, but I haven't come up with much, so I guess we'll have to leave it at that for now. Maybe more will come out later. Maybe during Chad Daybell's trial. I cannot wait!

CHAPTER 15:
THE COPS

By far, the most impressive thing about this case is the police. FBI; Rexburg, Idaho police; Gilbert, Arizona police; and Fremont and Madison County Sheriffs all worked together on this case. It could not have gone the way it did if they hadn't all worked in concert with each other.

We see in the movies the overbearing FBI agent who comes into small town America, shoving aside the inept local police and taking over the case. That was definitely not what happened here.

I had the privilege of sitting down for over an hour with Rexburg Detective Ray Hermosillo. Detective Hermosillo was the case detective, meaning he worked closely with the prosecution team as kind of a liaison between all of the different law enforcement agents and the prosecution.

I didn't know who he was when I first walked into the courtroom during jury selection, but he was there, he was hard to miss, and he would be there for every minute of the trial. There were several people who dedicated themselves to this case, but no one more than Detective Hermosillo.

Detective Hermosillo had been a Rexburg detective for only six months when his professional life would be turned upside down by Lori and Chad Daybell. He was first called into the case when Gilbert, Arizona police asked Rexburg, Idaho police for help tracking down the Jeep that was used in the attempted murder of Brandon Boudreaux. He had no idea at that time what was about to unfold.

"I'm glad I got to put evil away," he told me about his experience, when I asked him how he was doing. He says it is bittersweet after the sentencing, being able to see justice done but still having lingering emotions. He said the sights and smells are still burnt into his mind. "Evil touched everybody and ruined lives."

He wasn't able to answer some of my questions because the Chad Daybell trial hadn't happened yet, but we did have a great conversation and some of my questions were answered.

When I asked him if there was anything interesting that did not come up in the trial, he said he couldn't say because of the upcoming Chad Daybell trial. "It's so complex, sounds like something out of a movie," he said.

When I asked him if there would be anything new in the Chad Daybell trial, he said he couldn't get into specifics, but yes, there would be new information and they are still looking into leads.

I have been interested in whether or not the police are looking into the deaths of Joe Ryan and Alex Cox, thinking there must have been foul play in those deaths, but Detective Hermosillo says they are not looking into them. My own thought is that if they are not looking into them, it may be just because they have nothing solid to go on, no real evidence pointing to murder.

When the Rexburg police started questioning Lori Vallow Daybell, they initially had hope that the children were hidden away in a bunker or something. It makes sense, since Lori and Chad Daybell were preppers. It wasn't until Lori Daybell was given a court order to produce the children and she refused to comply or even respond, that the police began to suspect the children might already be dead.

I asked him if he thought anyone else was involved with the murders. Would anyone else be charged with crimes? I was thinking mostly of Melani Boudreax and Zulema Pastenes, but he said he didn't think so. I didn't really get an answer when I asked if he thought anyone else knew JJ and Tylee were dead.

He did answer yes when I asked if he thought it was Alex who shot at Tammy. I asked if the police had looked for shell casings or stray bullets and he explained that they hadn't considered it an attempted shooting until 6 months later when more evidence came in. By the time they realized it was a real gun and not a paintball gun, a lot of time had passed. They did go back and look for evidence (shell casings and bullets), but it was too late.

He talked a little bit about the jury. I hadn't realized, during the trial, how much we were being scrutinized. He said they were constantly trying to read the emotions on jurors' faces, but for the most part, we were pretty straight-faced. He did see a few head shakes during certain testimony, and of course there were some tears at times.

One of the biggest questions I have had during and since the trial is whether Lori Daybell is crazy or whether or not she believes what she says.

Det. Hermosillo: "I don't think Lori is crazy. She chooses to believe this stuff, but if you believe you've done nothing wrong, why are you hiding?"

He says she did know what she did, and she did believe her own BS that she had to cast out zombies. He says that she went down a rabbit hole of twisting and molding scripture.

The most intriguing answer I got was when I asked Detective Hermosillo this question:

"Do you think it was Alex seen entering Lori's storage unit on the video? It seems like some people think it was someone else, indicating that someone else might have been involved."

We had been shown a video in court of someone entering the storage unit that had been rented to Lori Ryan. In the video, we could only see the back of what appeared to be a man, but there was no way to tell who it was.

She had apparently used her name from a previous marriage to Joe Ryan when renting the unit. I make the assumption that she did that to throw the police off. That didn't work for a second, of course, but it points to how naive she was when it came to the investigative powers that would come into this case.

Anyway, Detective Hermosillo answered: "I know who it is but can't answer."

Interesting. Whoever it was, he was directly involved with the attempted shooting of Tammy and had knowledge of the contents of the storage unit: guns, Tylee and JJ's belongings, the camo gear worn by the shooter, and more. I guess we'll have to wait and hope we get the answer at Chad Daybell's trial.

When asked how he felt about Lori Daybell not getting a death sentence, he said he was torn. He initially wanted her to be sentenced to death because no punishment could possibly be enough, but as he thought about it, he realized life in prison might end up being more just. He says that Lori Daybell had said she would rather die, she welcomed her death. He thinks she is afraid of being in prison and what might happen to her there. Not only will she be subjected to her fellow inmates and what they may have in store for a mother who murdered her own children, but he hopes she will be confronted with the truth, that at some point the reality of what she did will come to her, and that would be justice for her.

I next asked him what he was thinking when Judge Boyce was making his statement leading up to the sentencing. I thought he would have been as nervous as I was listening to the portion of his statement where Judge Boyce was talking about what a model citizen Lori Daybell had been right up until she murdered Tammy, Tylee, and JJ. She had no record of any kind. He talked about how unusual that was and it sounded for a minute like he might use that as a reason to go easy on her.

Apparently though, Detective Hermosillo and all the other police officers involved had looked into Judge Boyce's prior sentencings and found that he had always been very methodical going through his thought processes leading up to the sentence he felt was most just. And, in the past, his sentencings had been pretty severe. Still, they had so much invested and must have been on pins and needles.

At this point in my interview with Detective Hermosillo, I quit asking questions and just let the conversation go where it would. I wanted to give him the opportunity to say whatever it might be that he would want to say, and I wasn't surprised to find that he did have some things to say.

He first wanted me to thank the rest of the jury, on his own behalf and the behalf of the entire law enforcement team involved in the case. He truly is thankful for the citizens who went through what we had to go through. The jurors, on the other hand, couldn't have been more impressed with the hard work and dedication on the part of the whole team of police, FBI, and the prosecution; even the defense. In other words, we were proud to see the system at its best.

Detective Hermosillo and I got a good chuckle talking about how it must have felt to be on the jury, going through the weeks of testimony, not knowing who the alternates would be, only to find out, at the very end, that I was an alternate. He asked what it felt like when my number was pulled out of the hat by the court clerk.

My response was mixed. My first thought was that I was stunned! By the end of the trial I had a definite opinion of what the verdict should be, and I was frustrated that I wouldn't get to be in that room deliberating just to make sure it went the right way.

My second thought was that I was a free man. For seven weeks I had been living nothing but this trial. I hadn't been allowed to talk to anyone about it. I still wouldn't be able to talk about it until the verdict was read, but still, what a relief!

He went on to talk about how it was hard to come into this case even as events were still unfolding but being 6 months behind. I hadn't thought about the fact that, by the time the police in Rexburg became involved in this case, it was 6 months old.

He talked more about trying to size up the jurors and guess where they stood. He described certain jurors to me and asked me questions about them.

Even though we jurors weren't allowed to talk about the case, we did certainly get to know each other. Without getting into specifics, I will say that I think he had the jurors pretty well pegged. Police officers make a living sizing people up and trying to figure out what's in their heads, and it was interesting hearing what he had to say about us. He might be interested to know that the jury was doing the same to him. He's a noticeable guy and I did overhear conversations about him.

He said that not only was he shocked to find himself involved in a case like this after only being a detective for 6 months, but he was even more shocked that something like this happened in Rexburg. "It's not supposed to happen here," he said. That led to a conversation about how outside influences are coming to Idaho.

Like it or not, things are changing. Idaho is growing so fast, mostly with people coming from California, Seattle, and Portland. Obviously they are coming to escape what is happening in those places and to live in a more civilized, safer community, but their coming here *is* going to change things.

He went on to talk about the small Rexburg Police Department and its lack of resources for investigating a case of this magnitude. They immediately called in the FBI to help. He was so impressed with how smoothly everyone worked together. He said the FBI, Arizona police, Rexburg police, and the Attorney General all worked in unison with no hiccups. He said they were all genuinely good people, and I thought that came through strongly in court. My thought was that if any case could shake the foundation of a community, a police department, or a police officer, it would be this one, but this community, this police department, and this police officer still seem to be standing on solid ground. I'm thankful for that.

We talked about how proud and hopeful that made us feel. He understands that the vast majority of people support the police and the hard work they do. He says he understands that "the ones who hate the police are the ones talking the most."

He talked about Lori Daybell's defense team, and he said they are really good people. In a small town, they all know each other, socialize together, and generally appreciate each other. I think that came through in the trial. There seemed to be a lot of respect on both sides.

He finished by reflecting on his career as a police officer and how he enjoys his job and wouldn't trade his experience as a police officer for anything.

I was glad to hear him say that after what he had just been through, but I could tell that he meant it. He should be proud, very proud of himself and his associates, and I think that that fact, more than anything, is what gets them through all the tough times.

We think it's us, the honest, law-abiding people supporting them, who enable them to deal with all the hard things they have to deal with, but I think it's themselves. I think it's the fraternity of police supporting each other. They're the ones who understand what it's like to do what they do. They're the ones who know what it's like to be beaten down while they are only trying to do the hard job of protecting us; seeing what they have to see, smelling the smells they have to smell, and then having to describe it all to us, hoping we'll get some sense of what it was like without damaging us too much.

Don't misunderstand me, we hold law enforcement to a higher standard, as we should. We expect them to keep their cool, hold fast to the law, give us all the benefit of the doubt. Too many times, they fall short of our expectations, and we make them pay the price. That is why, in this case, it felt so good to be able to fully and without any reservation say, "Good job folks, good job."

CHAPTER 16:
THE VICTIMS

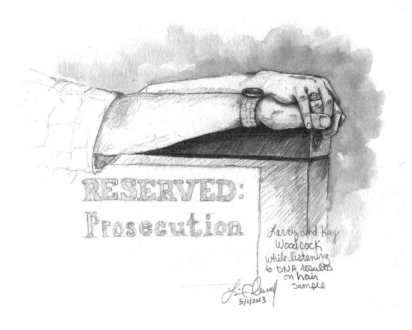

RESERVED: Prosecution

Larry and Kay
Woodcock
while listening
to DNA results
on hair
sample

5/1/2023

At the time of his death on July 11, 2019 in Chandler, Arizona, Lori Daybell's fourth husband, Leland Anthony "Charles" Vallow, was a 62-year-old businessman who made over $200,000 per year. Charles was born August 17, 1956 in Lake Charles, Louisiana. He loved the Austin, TX music scene and University of Texas football.

Charles and Lori Vallow moved to Kauai in 2014 and lived there until 2017, at which time they moved back to Arizona.

Charles had two sons, Cole and Zach, from a prior marriage, as well as Joshua Jackson, "JJ," who he adopted with Lori Vallow. He also adopted Tylee.

After the sentencing, I had the opportunity to meet Charles' brother, Gerry Vallow. I had never met Charles of course, but I've seen plenty of pictures and videos, and I have to say, Gerry and Charles look amazingly similar. Anyway, it was great to sit and listen to Gerry and his sister, Kay, talk about Charles. They seem to be such warm, sincere people, and it makes me think Charles must have been also.

I also got to talk to Gerry's wife, Melanie Vallow, on the phone about Charles. Since she is the third Melanie in this story, we'll call her Melanie V. She says she never liked Lori Vallow and she thought Charles was gullible. She thought Lori Vallow was greedy, self-centered, and superior, so she was not someone she wanted to get close to. Lori Vallow never took the time to visit or get to know Charles' family.

Melanie V. met Lori Daybell's father one time and his first words to her were, "You're not Catholic are you?" She says he was hyper religious and weird.

Melanie V. tells about how Charles helped Lori Vallow get an attorney to help with her custody battle with ex-husband Joe Ryan. Melanie V. thought Charles was being gullible, and she didn't believe the things Lori Vallow was saying about Joe.

She said, "You know she's lying to you, Charles," That upset Charles, and he was shocked that she would say that. Charles was so gentle, and Lori Vallow was so good at playing the victim.

When Melanie V. and Gerry confronted Charles and asked if he really believed that Joe did the things Lori Vallow was accusing him of, Charles replied, "No, he didn't believe it." Gerry asked, "Why couldn't you have married a normal woman?" But Gerry said Charles was so in love with her, he was in denial and just supported her no matter what.

Melanie V. says she thinks Chad Daybell is a Jim Jones wannabe and the catalyst in his and Lori Daybell's actions. Since more than 900 of Jim Jones' closest followers drank the "Kool Aid" and died from it, I can't understand how anyone would want to be like him, but I think she is right. He wanted to be the kind of leader people would follow even to their deaths.

When I spoke with her, Melanie V. also told me a story that gives us an important clue about Charles' murder. She said that she and Gerry went to Charles' apartment shortly after the murder and found that it had been cleared out of anything of value. Charles had several expensive watches that he was really proud of, and the watches and other things were missing. She thinks Lori Vallow Daybell had gone to the apartment and taken the items and sold them. This would have to have been done prior to Charles' murder, and she thinks it proves the murder was premeditated. We did hear testimony about this in court. Charles' grown kids asked Lori Vallow where the watches were and if she would send the watches to them. Lori Vallow agreed, but what the kids finally got, sometime later, after asking several more times, was a cheap Timex. This seemed super cold-hearted to me. She led them on for days and days and finally sent them something that seems to me to be more insulting than sympathetic.

Melanie V. also says Alex took Charles' truck and that Alex went off to Columbia on one of his sex junkets right after the murder. It will be interesting to see if this comes up in Lori Daybell's trial in Arizona. I will explain more about her trial in Arizona in Chapter 24.

According to Gerry, he and Charles were close growing up. Charles was less than a year and a half older. There were 6 children in the Vallow family, 3 boys and 3 girls. There was another child that died as a baby. They all grew up in Lake Charles, Louisiana. Childhood was good for Charles. As was typical for most families in the '60s and '70s, they didn't have a lot of extra money. Of course there were no smartphones or laptops and just a few channels on TV.

Charles was just one year older than I am, and I can imagine exactly what his childhood was like. Times were simpler and more innocent then. Yeah, we didn't have a lot of the things kids have today, but we had something kids these days don't have: freedom. And I wouldn't trade freedom for all the gadgets and comforts in the world.

It's really hard to explain what that was like to kids growing up now. Yeah, I can talk about it, I can describe it, but I can't give them the sense of excitement, security, and the fun we had. Days were filled with wiffle ball, baseball, and swimming in the summer; football in the street and basketball in the driveway the rest of the year. We would ride our bikes for miles, exploring. I think our moms thought we were riding around the neighborhood, but we could have been anywhere.

We didn't have helmets or knee pads, but what we did have was a sense of invincibility based on toughness, independence, and a sense that our group of friends was bigger, stronger, and tougher than anyone or anything we might encounter.

On summer evenings, everyone would come outside after dinner. No one had air conditioning and it felt great to get out of the hot house and into the cooler air as the sun went down. Kids would be playing hide and go seek or kick the can.

When we got to high school, it was Friday night football and cruising the main in someone's mom's car. If it was equipped with FM radio, we would blast some of the best music ever created.

I wonder, is it better to be comfortable on your couch watching anything you can imagine on TV or YouTube in the perfectly conditioned, filtered air, or was it better when everyone knew their neighbors well because they spent so much time outside?

No contest as far as I'm concerned, and I've experienced both. I wouldn't trade my childhood for what we have today for anything.

I recommend *The Sandlot, The Wonder Years,* and *Dazed and Confused* if you want to get an idea or maybe re-live those years.

Charles was a pitcher on his high school baseball team, and he must have been good. He struck out 13 batters in his first game as a freshman and he was on his way to a minor league contract when he blew out his shoulder. Prior to his injury, he had been pursued by the Yankees and the Astros.

What's more important to know about Charles is what kind of person he was. Lori Vallow Daybell says he was threatening and mean to her and her kids.

After talking to his family, I know this can't be true. He was kind, generous, and always giving of himself. He was the protector of anyone who might need protection, but not in a forceful or violent way. He was the friendly, kindhearted, gentle soul and funny jock who everyone loved. Gerry says he never had a mean bone in his body.

Charles loved kids and kids loved him. He was JJ's protector and supporter in every way he could be. One of his favorite things to do was to take kids camping and introduce them to fishing.

One of the stories Gerry told me about his brother Charles was of a time when Gerry was being bullied relentlessly in school. Gerry finally told Charles about it and asked for his help when Charles noticed his black eye. He was tired of the black eyes and bruises.

A day later Charles came to Gerry and told him he "took care of his problem with the bully." Gerry wondered how Charles accomplished this. He imagined Charles must have taken care of it in the way we would expect, but he found out some time later that the bully's sister had a crush on Gerry. Charles had talked to the sister and the sister somehow stopped her brother from bullying Gerry. Charles had found a non-violent way of solving the problem, and that is who Charles is.

Gerry tells another story of when he was pitching a playoff game in Little League baseball. Apparently Gerry really stunk it up, allowing the other team to win. It was the only game Gerry's team had lost all season. The team had high hopes going into that game and the loss ended the season. Gerry was humiliated and defeated.

When the game was finally over and it was time to go home their mom said, "Boys, get in the car."

But Charles said, "Mom, me and Gerry will be walking home."

On the walk home, as they threw rocks and kicked cans down the street, Charles consoled Gerry telling him of a quote he had heard, saying something like "it's better to have played and lost than never to have played."

Gerry says it didn't really help at the time, but he did appreciate the fact that his brother, who he looked up to, took the time to try, and that did make him feel better. Gerry tells these stories much better than I do in his Southern drawl, but you get the idea.

Getting to know Charles through his family makes me furious at Lori Daybell, and I can only imagine the anger his family is feeling.

The last thing Gerry told me is that he can't wait for the trial in Arizona. He wants to see Lori Daybell convicted of murdering his brother, and he is already thinking about the victim impact statement he will give at her sentencing.

Before marrying Charles, Lori Ryan was flat broke, barely able to provide for her children. Charles took great care of Lori Vallow and her family. He built Lori Vallow a beauty salon and a dance studio in his house so she would have something to do even though they didn't need the income.

In court we listened to Chad Daybell's call to the funeral home the day after Charles died, using a false name and asking for a price for cremation and shipping Charles' cremains from Chandler, Arizona to New Orleans, Louisiana.

In the call, we could clearly hear Chad Daybell lie, spelling out his name as Chad Dabal and saying he was Charles' nephew from Iowa. He had originally given his name as Chad Daybell, but it seemed like he had second thoughts and decided to change it to Dabal.

It felt really creepy hearing Chad Daybell say he was "sorry to see him [Charles] go." He claimed he was calling on behalf of the family who, he said, wanted Charles' body cremated and the cremains shipped to New Orleans. It was actually Chad and Lori Daybell who wanted Charles cremated, not Charles' family. The family had no idea that Chad Daybell was calling the funeral home "on their behalf."

I think Chad Daybell and Lori Vallow must have wanted Charles cremated in order to avoid an autopsy, which may be an indication that Charles was already incapable of being a threat after he was shot the first time. He could not have been a threat as he was laying on his back on the floor with the first bullet through his chest. At least that was my assumption after listening to the tape of the phone call in court. This is very important because it would be the difference between possible self-defense for Alex and murder. It also indicates that the murder was planned and Lori Vallow was lying to police to cover it up. Alex could have quit after the first shot and called 911. He could also have given Charles CPR while waiting for the EMTs to show up which could possibly have saved Charles' life. Instead, he waited 45 minutes to call it in. Was he waiting for Charles to bleed out? I think so. I'm sure it will all come out in Lori Daybell's trial in Arizona.

In court, we also listened to and watched body cam footage of Charles pleading with the police about 6 months before he died. He told police that Lori Vallow thought she was married to the angel Moroni and that Charles was actually a zombie named Nick Schneider. She had said the only way to save him (Charles) was to murder him. It was very sad to watch him plead with the police. Charles was a big guy and he seemed terrified and desperate for help.

The police in Arizona didn't ignore Charles. They went to Lori Vallow's hotel to confront her, but she wasn't there. Charles had paid for a hotel for Lori Vallow because they weren't getting along. Even though she didn't want to live with him, he still felt obligated to provide for her.

Lori Vallow ended up voluntarily admitting herself into Community Bridges Mental Health Facility before the police could catch up with her, but apparently she buffaloed the people there too, as she was released only four hours later. She told people there that Charles was cheating on her and abusive to her and her children and really sounded sincere as she justified her actions to them. Of course, we know the opposite was true. Lori Vallow was the one cheating and there is no indication that Charles had ever cheated on his wife or harmed her or the children.

Detective Nathan Duncan of the Chandler, Arizona Police Department testified about Charles, and it was extremely revealing in terms of how far Lori Vallow and Chad Daybell were willing to go, and what lies they were willing to tell to get what they wanted. They had no remorse or regard for anyone else whatsoever.

Detective Duncan was able to access Chad Daybell's and Lori Vallow's email accounts. In one email Lori Vallow claims to be Charles asking Chad Daybell to come to Arizona to act as a ghostwriter for a book he was supposedly writing. It was an obvious ploy to give Chad Daybell an excuse to come to Arizona to see Lori Vallow, without Chad Daybell's wife, Tammy, knowing the truth.

It was extremely interesting to learn how police gained access to texts and emails associated with Chad and Lori Daybell. The Daybells had used 9 "burner" phones thinking police wouldn't be able to track them. The use of even one burner phone is typically evidence of guilt, let alone 9.

It was very much over my head listening to how that was done, but the gist of it was that the police were able to subpoena the text messages from the phone server, and messages are stored by the phone server on the cloud, where the police could access them.

If someone using a burner phone accessed their email or anything else in the cloud, the information in the burner phone could be retrieved by the police once they had a warrant. Once they concluded a phone had been used by one of the two, they could access all the content. And there was a ton of content. Police had to go through it all to find texts and emails pertinent to the case. They had to have spent hundreds if not thousands of hours doing this. We were presented with hours and hours of it in court, and they said it was just a very small percentage.

Also, Lori Daybell had several email accounts using different names and they had to find them all and prove they belonged to her. It was sometimes monotonous, but also very interesting testimony. It also revealed how naive Lori and Chad Daybell were to the powers of the police to find the evidence they needed. Or they just thought they were smarter than the police.

I thought to myself that anyone would have made the same mistakes. I was completely unaware that they could do these things. They used cell towers to triangulate and find out where Alex was and exactly when he was there. This is how they found the locations of JJ and Tylee's graves. They found that Alex was at the pond under the tree in Chad Daybell's backyard.

Some of the email accounts Lori Vallow Daybell used were "Lori4style@icloud.com" and "Lollytimeforever@gmail.com." We know Lori Vallow Daybell was into fashion, hair styles, clothes, etc., and that her sister who died as a baby was Lolly.

Detective Duncan also gained access to Lori Vallow's texts between her and her then husband Charles. In Charles' texts to Lori Vallow, you can hear him pleading with her and trying to make sense of what she was doing. Lori Vallow not only took his life, but she put him through hell before finally murdering him.

This was the man who literally saved her and her children from poverty and gave them all a great life. A beautiful home, good schools, and everything they might need. According to accounts, they were extremely well provided for by Charles. Not only that, but Charles was a catch. Friends called him handsome, fun to be around, and loving. As we have seen, he had been a jock and was still very fit at the time of his death.

Before allegedly brutally murdering Charles, Lori Vallow drained his business account, locked him out of his house, canceled his return flight, and took his vehicle out of the airport parking lot while Charles was on a business trip. She went on to accuse him of cheating on her and being abusive, an accusation countered by Colby Ryan's testimony. It's unclear to me why she did this. It is usually some ego injury that causes a narcissist to do something like this, but I don't know what Charles might have done to her. It looks like he did absolutely nothing so maybe it was just her plan to hurt him.

On the witness stand Colby said Charles was the only real father he had ever had, and that Charles was good to him, treating him like his own son. Colby was and is furious with his mother, trying to make sense of what she did. He lost the only father he ever had, his sister and brother who he loved, and his mother, and is doing his best to go on with his life in as normal a way as possible. I can't imagine how he can do that, but I hope he finds his way.

Draining his business account caused all kinds of havoc for Charles. He wasn't able to pay his employees or business bills, so he was being sued. Listening to the testimony in court, I couldn't help feeling very sorry for Charles. He thought he had met his dream woman when he asked Lori Ryan to marry him. He truly loved her and her kids.

After listening to all the testimony and watching all the video, I really don't think Lori Vallow had Charles murdered for any other reason than that she wanted the life insurance money she thought she would get when he died. She was that cold hearted. That's what's so hard to understand, but it's the only conclusion I can come to after seeing all the evidence and seeing firsthand her reaction to it in court. If she pushed Charles out of her life, she would lose his financial support, but if she murdered him and got away with it, she thought she would be rich.

Getting to know Charles through his family has really helped me to understand what actually happened in this case. There are so many layers, so much deception, and it's extremely hard to understand.

Were the victims good people? Was Charles mean to Tylee? Can we believe Colby's testimony about Charles? Did Charles contribute to his own murder by coming into Lori Vallow's house with a confrontational attitude? Did he provoke Alex?

I wasn't sure about any of this when the trial ended. You know the saying, "it takes two." Well, I am sure now that Charles came into Lori Vallow's house just to pick up JJ. Possibly he was excited to see Lori Vallow and maybe still hoping for a chance to reconcile their relationship. I don't believe he did anything to excuse what Alex and Lori Vallow did to him, and I don't think he had any idea of the danger he was walking into. I don't think he knew Alex would be there. I think he was "bushwhacked," as they used to say.

After talking to Charles' brother, Gerry, and others who were close to Charles, I now better understand Charles' relationship with Tylee, which, in turn, helps me to understand Tylee. Charles was a great father to Tylee. He provided a good stable home for her. He loved her as if she was his own daughter. He even helped her buy her Jeep.

But what about Chad Daybell? Was he so cold hearted? Would he murder his spouse just for his own selfish reasons? He absolutely was. So, somehow these two unbelievably selfish, narcissistic human beings found each other.

There have been murderous couples in the past. According to an article in *Next Luxury* by Tobias Handke, there have been several serial killer couples who have bonded over their love of torture and murder.

It was Christmas Eve, 1995, in Ontario, Canada. Tammy Homolka (don't confuse her with Tammy Daybell) was enjoying the eggnog and rum her sister Karla and Karla's husband, Paul Bernardo, were feeding her. Upstairs, Tammy and Karla's parents were hosting a dinner party.

Tammy was a student at the Sir Winston Churchill Secondary School where she played soccer and ran on the track team. She was just a week away from her 16th birthday. Karla and Paul were a very good-looking couple. Tammy was enjoying the attention of the popular pair and feeling a little naughty drinking the alcohol.

Little did she know that her sister and her sister's husband had laced her drink with valium. The couple had been planning this night for a while. In fact, they had been fantasizing about raping 15-year-old Tammy.

Paul had been disappointed to find out on their wedding night that Karla was not a virgin, and he held that against her.

Karla thought she could make up for this by allowing Paul to have sex with her sister. Apparently the two enjoyed pretending that Karla was Tammy while having sex. Karla would say: *"My name is Tammy, I'm 15 years old. I'm a virgin and I want to marry you."*

After the valium took effect, the couple carried Tammy to the basement where they both raped her. Paul first and then Karla at Paul's insistence. They recorded the event with Paul's video camera.

After raping her, they placed a cloth soaked in the anesthetic Halothane, which Karla had stolen from the animal hospital where she worked, over Tammy's mouth. Tammy started to vomit and choke. The couple called 911 but they were too late. Tammy suffocated to death at the hands of her older sister and her brother-in-law.

Unfortunately the police initially thought Tammy had died of alcohol poisoning, and Paul and Karla were free to carry on.

Sometime later Paul beat Karla, and to get back at him, Karla struck a deal with authorities describing how her and husband Paul raped her virginal 15-year-old sister Tammy and left her to die. She told police that after marrying, Paul discovered Karla wasn't a virgin. To make up for that they raped Tammy and left her tied up in bed while they went to sleep in their own bed. She went on to tell how they filmed themselves raping and torturing Tammy's inert body, and how Tammy ended up choking to death on her own vomit.

After they brutally raped and murdered Tammy and before Karla went to the police, the couple went on to repeat their grotesque actions twice, killing 15-year-old Leslie Mahaffy and 15-year-old Kristen French. They were dubbed the Ken and Barbie killers.

Karla ended up serving 12 years in prison and is free now. Paul is serving a life sentence but is eligible for parole.

Another killer couple: According to an article by Richard Stockton, Gerald and Charlene Gallego murdered at least 10 people between 1978 and 1980 in the Sacramento, California area.

On September 11, 1978, 17-year-old Rhonda Sheffler and 16-year-old Kippi Vaught were shopping in a Sacramento mall when they were approached by Charlene. Charlene offered them pot and lured them into her van. Once inside the two girls were confronted by Gerald who had a gun pointed at them. Charlene drove them into the Sierra Nevada Mountains where Gerald raped them before shooting them in the head.

Rhonda and Kippi were the couple's first known rape and murder victims, but they would go on to repeat this scenario several times. Another of their victims, a 21-year-old hitchhiker named Linda Aguilar, was visibly pregnant when she was picked up by Gerald and Charlene. Still, they raped, strangled, and bludgeoned her, and buried her alive.

The rest of their victims would be bound, raped, and murdered and their bodies would be dumped in remote areas of the Sierra Nevada Mountains.

This couple had an extremely checkered past. Gerald's father had been executed in a Mississippi prison for shooting and killing a prison guard, and Gerald had already been convicted of armed robbery before meeting Charlene.

Charlene had been married twice before and had a history of crime and violence.

Similarly, Alton Coleman and Debra Brown raped and murdered their way across the country in 1984, targeting children. Coleman was executed in 2002 and Brown got 140 years.

Then there was 19-year-old Charles Starkweather and 14-year-old Caril Ann Fugate, who killed at least 11 people, starting with a gas station attendant who they robbed before moving on to Fugate's parents and a baby sister.

Bonnie and Clyde Barrow are probably the most famous killer couple, but they pale in comparison to some.

Murderous couples are not unprecedented. We have seen it many times in the past. It's scary enough when one murderer is on the loose. When you put two of them together, it's even more terrifying because it is so much easier for them to dupe and overpower their victims.

One thing most of these couples seem to have in common after finally being caught is that the female half always claims the male half forced her. Even though, in the case of Gerald and Charlene Gallego, Charlene had left bite marks on her victims.

This is not something we see in the case of Chad and Lori Daybell. I'm sure the prosecution must have been worried that Lori Daybell would claim Chad Daybell was the mastermind and used Lori Daybell, but that did not happen. I know that, as I sat in court, I thought the defense would surely use that argument at some point in the trial. In fact, Lori Daybell would not allow her defense team to use that defense.

I can easily see how they could have done it. Lori Daybell is a master manipulator and if they could have somehow gotten her good looks back to what they were before she was arrested, she could have used her charm on the jury. I like to think that would not have worked on me, but it certainly had worked on a lot of other people prior to her arrest. I do have to think that, by the time the case came to trial, it was hopeless for Lori Daybell and her defense team, regardless of her looks and charms. *Everyone* was on to her by this point and the prosecution was doing a great job of making it hard for the defense to do or say anything that might sway the jury. Lori Daybell was as cold blooded a killer as she could possibly be and could turn on and attack her victim as quickly and decisively as a wolf.

Back to Chad Daybell and his murdered wife, Tammy. Tammy was a mother of five children and three grandchildren with another on the way when she was murdered in her bed.

According to her obituary she was born in May 1970 in Pasadena, California. She loved living close to Disneyland and was a gifted student at Cerritos Elementary School. At the age of 13, she moved with her family to Springville, Utah where she was a member of her high school band, yearbook editor, and was liked by everyone. She created her own library and lent books to her siblings using actual library cards and fines when the books weren't returned on time.

Tammy went on to attend Brigham Young University where she met Chad Daybell the summer after her freshman year. They quickly fell in love and married on March 9, 1990 in the Manti Temple. While Chad finished college, Tammy supported the family by working for the Springville Parks Department.,

As the family grew, Tammy became a stay-at-home mom until they moved back to Springville where she took a job as the computer teacher at Art City Elementary School.

In 2004, Tammy and Chad Daybell started the Spring Creek Book Company, mostly publishing Chad Daybell's religious books. In 2015, the family moved to Salem, Idaho, and Tammy became the librarian at Madison Middle School and later at Central Elementary School in Salem, Idaho. She was also Stake Girls Camp director and Relief Society President in the Church of Jesus Christ of Latter-Day Saints. She loved gardening, pets, and cooking.

For those of us who didn't know Tammy, these details are important. It's too easy to make assumptions about anyone involved with someone like Chad Daybell. It's easy to think people's lives are a mess, but in Tammy's case we see a woman of value to everyone around her. She was truly loved by her family, students, co-workers and friends. In fact, I think she was so good-hearted that she didn't see her murder by her husband coming at all.

She even thought that Alex, wearing a mask and camo gear and shooting at her practically point blank with a semi-automatic rifle, had been just a kid pranking her with a paintball gun. I don't think she ever did think anything different. Sadly, maybe the truth was just too terrifying for her to acknowledge.

It was dark and Tammy had just come home from shopping. She had parked her car in the driveway, gotten out, and was in the process of getting bags of groceries out of the backseat when a man approached her wearing a mask and camo gear. The man shot at her from close range two times. The rifle wouldn't have sounded loud like a normal rifle because it was equipped with a suppressor. According to what she told police following the incident, she thought it had been a paintball gun. Still, it must have been terrifying for her.

But how could Alex have missed at such a close range? Less than a car length away? Did he "chicken out" and miss on purpose, or was he just a terrible shot? We'll never know.

It must have been a horrible shock to her waking up, after going to bed feeling safe at home with her husband, to find herself being smothered to death!

Also, how many people were involved in Tammy's murder? According to her husband, Chad Daybell, she had died in her sleep in bed. He claimed she had been sick the night before and he woke up shocked and distraught to find her dead in their bed.

It seemed to me, listening to the medical examiner describe the bruising on Tammy's exhumed body, that there would have been more bruising. She would have put up more of a fight. The only way I can see that she had so little bruising would have been if she were being held down by someone while someone else was holding whatever it was they used to asphyxiate her over her face. So, at least two people, and I would think more likely two people holding her while another person asphyxiated her.

Who was there? Another question we'll never get the answer to, but it makes me extremely suspicious of the other characters involved with Chad Daybell's cult.

Also, even though Tammy supported her husband Chad Daybell's book writing career, and his books were all about the "end of days" and the second coming of Christ, it doesn't seem like she was actually a part of his cult. She isn't mentioned as being involved in the podcasts or the casting out of spirits. Tammy was simply a good wife, mother, grandmother, co-worker, and teacher of children. She was a good Mormon. She did not deserve in any way what happened to her. She should have been cherished and protected by her husband. She earned that and deserved it. In her way, she is as innocent as Tylee and JJ.

To me, Tylee is the saddest character in this story. Tylee was a 16-year-old girl just getting started in life. She was born September 24, 2002 in Phoenix, Arizona to parents Joseph and Lori Ryan, and died on September 8, 2019 in Rexburg, Idaho. She was simply a teenage girl doing the typical things a teenage girl would be doing, probably looking forward to her upcoming birthday.

Beyond that she was her brother JJ's protector and caregiver. As we know, JJ was a young boy with severe autism, and was a handful to say the least. Sister Tylee was always there for him and truly loved taking care of him. She truly loved his energy and his antics. In fact, it seems that JJ's mom, Lori Vallow Daybell, was self-absorbed and not as involved with JJ as a mom should have been, so Tylee was a blessing. According to people close to Tylee, she didn't want to move to Idaho and leave her life in Arizona, but she did so to stay with JJ.

It was hard for Tylee to maintain friends because she was moved around a lot. She did have one good friend who tried to stay in contact with Tylee after she moved to Idaho. This friend, who I won't name here, tried to text Tylee and got only strange, short texts in return. We were shown these texts in court and I thought they were pretty damning considering Lori Daybell had been insisting she knew where the kids were, and they were okay. It turns out that Tylee was already dead and buried and the replies the friend was getting were most likely from Lori Daybell using Tylee's phone and pretending to be Tylee. Someone had to have sent them, and Lori Daybell was the one who had Tylee's phone.

Stepfather Charles Vallow had helped Tylee buy a Jeep which we were told she loved. Tylee made the payments on the Jeep with the money she got from the Social Security death benefit from her father, Joe Ryan. It turns out that it was the same Jeep Alex drove to Arizona and used in the attempted shooting of Brandon Boudreaux. This, of course, is after he had murdered Tylee.

We were shown pictures of the Jeep in court. We were also shown pictures of Lori Daybell and a man the police think was Alex Cox at Lori Daybell's storage unit around the time of the attempted murder on Brandon. The police had found guns, camo gear, facemasks, and the spare tire from the Jeep among other things in the storage unit. Lori Daybell had used the name Lori Ryan when renting the unit. The police found a receipt in Lori Daybell's apartment for the storage unit and got a warrant to search it.

I think this is indicative of how stupid and arrogant Lori Daybell was. How could she not think the police would find the receipt and search the storage unit? How could she have been so careless to leave the receipt laying around? I would have loved for her to have gotten on the stand to testify on her own behalf, and answer questions like these.

The last "proof of life" we have of Tylee was the picture taken by Lori Daybell of her, JJ, and Uncle Alex in Yellowstone on September 8, 2019. When the police became suspicious about Tylee and JJ's whereabouts, the police kept asking Lori Daybell for proof of life since she refused to produce the children and kept saying they were safe and being protected. The police hoped that was true at the time but were skeptical since she wouldn't produce anything that would prove they were still alive.

What makes Tylee a sadder character than Charles, Tammy, or even JJ? I think she had an idea of what was coming. I think Lori Vallow had mentally abused her her whole life.

I had to think a lot about Tylee in order to come to a conclusion about her. We have the strange police video after Charles' murder where she seems so unaffected by what had happened, and she seems to support her mother's story, which she had to have known was untrue. But why would she do that? Why would she say

Charles had been threatening and had forcefully taken the bat away from her? Remember, according to Tylee and Lori Vallow's account of the event to police, given right after Charles was shot by Alex, Tylee had heard Charles shouting and threatening her mom, and had come out of her room with the bat to protect her. Charles then took the bat from her and turned-on Alex, precipitating Alex's use of the gun to defend himself.

Mentally abusing a child can be done in many ways. Imagine a baby just beginning to crawl and move around, sitting on a blanket. The parent puts something attractive to the baby just off the blanket. Of course, the baby is going to try to get to the attractive thing. It could be a toy or some food, it doesn't matter, just something the baby is going to try to get to. When the baby crawls off the blanket to get to the object, the baby is punished and put back on the blanket. The punishment could be spanking, slapping, pinching, or anything that causes pain. The baby is taught not to go after the object of his or her desire, but to stay on the blanket where it is safe.

Imagine a child who is taught that anything outside of the mother-child relationship is dangerous. Imagine a child who is taught to smile and act happy or else pain will be inflicted at some later point.

This child would end up being an empty shell only existing to serve the mother.

Now, imagine years and years of this kind of conditioning and you can imagine the effect it would have. The abuse doesn't have to be as clear as this example. It's the parent teaching the child not to explore; exploring is dangerous. The parent is the controlling factor. The result is that the child is fearful of the parent and will do what the parent wants. The child will even try to predict what the parent expects in order to avoid the punishment from the parent. At some point, the parent no longer has to punish the child. Just the threat is enough, so the relationship between the parent and child might look normal to everyone else. The child might look normal, but the fact is that the child is damaged and will carry this conditioning through his or her entire life.

This explains why we see how Tylee seemed to protect her mother. Tylee was likely tortured by Lori Vallow. Another victim who is so innocent, she wasn't in any way aware of what her mom was capable of. And, just as we have seen with Tammy, the truth would be too terrifying to acknowledge.

We were shown a video of Tylee and Lori Vallow being interviewed by the police after Charles' murder. Tylee seems to back up Lori Vallow's story of what happened. Why would she do that? She was there the morning of the murder.

Tylee said she was asleep in her room when she was awakened by yelling. She said she came out of her room with a baseball bat and confronted Charles, trying to protect her mother from him. Charles took the bat from her and supposedly used it on Alex. Alex did have a small cut on the back of his head that was bleeding slightly when the police showed up.

On the police video, we saw Alex using a rag to supposedly soak up the blood, but he was obviously overusing the rag and barely bleeding. Charles was a big guy, and remember, he had been a potential minor league baseball player. If he had hit Alex, it must have been just a tap or surely Alex would have been more severely wounded.

Here is the text of the 911 call Alex made about 45 minutes after shooting Charles:

Nine one one, where is your emergency?
It's at 5531 South Four Peaks Lane.
What's the emergency there?
I got in a fight with my brother-in-law, and I shot him in self-
defense.

Okay, let me get medics on the phone. Is he hurt? Is he alive?
Yeah, there's blood. He's not moving. I shot my brother-in-law.
What happened there?
He came at me with a bat. I've never seen him that enraged before.

When the police showed up at the house, the operator asked Alex to walk outside with his hands in the air. Officer Irwin Wierzbicki was there waiting for him. Officer Wierzbicki checked him for weapons and told him to sit on the curb.

Officer Wierzbicki then went into the house and found Charles laying in a puddle of blood. Two .45 caliber casings were laying on the floor and Charles had no pulse.

When Lori Vallow came back, and she and Tylee were questioned by the police, Lori Vallow told them she had sent Tylee to the car to watch JJ after Charles took the bat away, so Tylee wasn't in the house when Alex shot Charles.

The police video of Lori Vallow and Tylee was bizarre to say the least. Neither were in the least visibly upset. In fact, they were laughing and joking with the police.

Lori Vallow claimed that Charles never liked Tylee and was mean to her. Even if the things they said about Charles were true, they should have been affected by what had happened that morning. But both seem relaxed and had a story that now doesn't ring at all true. Sitting in court, I had no idea of what Charles and Tylee's relationship was like, but I know now, after talking to people who knew Charles and Tylee, that Charles was very good to Tylee and in fact was one of the few adults in her daily life that she could have depended on. She must have felt, after Charles died, that she was left with wolves. She must have been terrified.

I have thought a lot about Tylee, and I just think that innocent, 16-year-old Tylee was willing to do or say whatever Lori Vallow told her to. I don't think she knew at the time that her mom was a

murderer, although she must have been catching on after Charles'
death. I think she was manipulated by her mom and made to
think things that weren't true. I think her reaction to Charles'
death was practiced and rehearsed, coached by Lori Vallow.

Tylee was tormented by her mom. She was 16 years old at the
time of her death. A tough age. She must have struggled trying to
come to terms with her mother's actions. I think she was probably
beginning to be afraid of her mother and what she might be
capable of. She would have been defenseless and at the mercy of
her mother.

It does show how manipulative Lori Vallow is. She would
use anyone, even her own daughter, to hide the truth. Half-
truths, manipulation, fear, and a constant barrage of it all, is what
it would have taken to make Tylee act the way she acted after
Charles' death.

In court, we heard a taped phone conversation where Lori
Vallow called Tylee dark. We could hear Tylee in the background
saying, "Not me, mom, I'm not dark."

Tylee's remains were found by police on June 9, 2020 in a
shallow grave in Chad Daybell's backyard in Rexburg, Idaho.

The description below is going to be hard for you to read so
feel free to skip over it to the next chapter. We had to see a lot in
court that you didn't see if you were following the trial. I am not
trying to sensationalize the story or shock you, but I think it is
important for you to know how brutal the deaths of both JJ and
Tylee were, and what the police and FBI agents had to go through
to find Tylee and JJ.

As you read on, you will find that I count these police officers
as some of Chad and Lori Daybell's victims. No amount of
hardness gained by their experience in law enforcement could have
prepared them for what they found. I don't think that listening to
the testimony and seeing the pictures will ever leave me. How

must it have affected them, seeing the remains of Tylee and JJ firsthand?

In court, the defense argued to not let the pictures of JJ and Tylee's remains be shown. We had to listen to "white noise" as we watched the defense, the prosecution, and Judge Boyce talk it over. Judge Boyce decided that the pictures would be shown to the jury. I looked at Lori Daybell while the pictures were put up on the screen. She was as slumped in her chair as she could be, looking away from the screen with her head down.

I found out after the trial was over that the defense team had also argued to let Lori Daybell out of the courtroom while the pictures were shown, but thankfully, Judge Boyce didn't allow her to get out of that.

How did police find the graves? Through cell phone location, they knew that Alex had been in Chad Daybell's backyard around the time they suspected the murders to have occurred. They knew he had spent a lot of time by the dry pond.

There was also an area they knew to be what the Daybell family called their pet cemetery. There was a burned area and evidence that the ground had been disturbed. When they started digging, they were expecting to find a body buried there. What they found was a green bucket mostly burned or melted.

At first the police weren't sure what they had found, but inside the bucket and in the surrounding soil they found what they believed to be burned human tissue and bone. Buried under the bucket they found what they believed to be what was left of a human skull. They couldn't immediately identify it as human, but they were sure it was the remains of Tylee. They also found some jewelry and what appeared to be human teeth.

It was extremely hard and one of our worst days in court listening to Rexburg Detective Ray Hermosillo and others testify about what they found and how her body had been "rendered."

We had to sit there and look at the pictures presented by the prosecution showing what they found. I know I felt terrible for the people who had to go through this in real life and I'm sure the other jurors felt the same.

We were shown pictures of a melted green bucket, what looked like burned or melted tissue and pieces of bone, one that was obviously a jawbone. We saw pictures of the remnants of jewelry that matched with jewelry that Tylee owned. We were shown pictures of bone that had been struck by something like a pick or ax. We were also shown pictures of the pick and shovel found in Chad Daybell's barn that turned out to have material with Tylee's DNA on it.

It seemed to me that the prosecution was insinuating that Tylee had been beaten with these implements while she was still alive, but they didn't come right out and make that accusation. I think it would have been hard to prove anyway, given the condition of her body.

Things were horrible enough and I was left wondering what Tylee had to go through at the hands of Uncle Alex. Did she know what was coming? Did she know her own mom conspired to have her brutally murdered? We'll never know, but I'll never stop wondering.

What there was of her remains were sent to the FBI lab in Quantico, Virginia along with the pick, shovel, machete, ax or hatchet, and some other tools. Her death was determined to be "homicide by unspecified means." This is a term that is used when investigators can't determine which of the injuries killed the victim.

I am deeply saddened and angered thinking about Tylee's death and her life. I think she might have known what was coming and that's what makes me the saddest. I don't think JJ would have known until it was actually happening to him, which is in itself horrible to think about, but at least he didn't have to live in fear of his mom.

Even though Charles knew at some point what Lori Vallow Daybell was capable of, he was a 62-year-old man and would have been better equipped to deal with his fears than a 16-year-old girl. I think Tylee's mom caused her to live in fear until she murdered her. I think her mom manipulated her and mentally abused her her whole life and I think her mom was cunning enough to get away with it without anyone noticing.

In a September, 2022 EastIdahoNews report, Nate Eaton stated that Tylee and JJ's bodies had still not been released to the family. In the article, Larry Woodcock, Tylee and JJ's grandfather, is reported to have said, "All I want to do is bury the kids. It's been three years. JJ's in a vault right here in town. He's in a freezer. Come on, judge, let us have him so we can bury him."

As of this writing, I can't find anything more recent so I'm guessing the bodies are still being held as evidence until the Chad Daybell trial is over. *(Note: JJ and Tylee's remains were both held at Madison Memorial Hospital in Rexburg. JJ's remains were released to Larry and Kay on October 16, 2023. On December 21, 2023 Judge Boyce also released Tylee's remains.)*

Hopefully the family can finally put them to rest as soon as that is over.

Lori Daybell makes JJ out to have been some kind of monster, literally. She said he was climbing on the refrigerator and cabinets. She claimed he was possessed by a demon.

The last "proof of life" we have of JJ is the picture of him on the couch at home sadly wearing the same red pajamas the police found his body in when they exhumed him in Chad Daybell's backyard on June 9, 2020.

JJ was born on May 25, 2012 in Chandler, Arizona to parents Mandy Leger, now deceased, and Todd Trahan. JJ's biological

parents both suffered from substance abuse and JJ was fostered by Todd Trahan's parents, Larry and Kay Woodcock, who were also Charles Vallow's sister and brother in law. In 2013 JJ was adopted by Lori and Charles Vallow.

Larry and Kay petitioned for custody of JJ, hoping to keep him with them in Louisiana. Even though they knew Larry and Kay loved JJ more than anything and would have done anything for him, Child Protective Services sided with Charles and Lori Vallow.

Apparently Child Protective Services thought this would be a more suitable arrangement for JJ, and Charles and Lori Vallow were both happy to take on the challenges associated with raising a child with autism.

If you listen to Lori Daybell talk about JJ, you would think he was a negative force in people's lives. She makes him sound mean, overactive, and destructive with a negative energy.

Kay, Larry, Colby, and Tylee don't describe him that way at all. They loved his energy and said he was positive and happy. They loved having JJ in their lives and he was in no way a problem. They thought of him as a blessing.

We know Tylee spent a lot of time with JJ and it was her own choice to do so. Colby says he would have taken JJ and raised him. We know Larry and Kay would have taken him back and raised him. I'm sure any number of families in Rexburg would have been willing to raise him. Larry believes JJ would have gone on to do great things with his life if it hadn't been snatched away from him.

JJ's biological mother, Mandy, felt extremely guilty about losing JJ and spent the rest of her life working toward getting free of drugs and getting JJ back. Apparently she died in 2022 of complications due to hypertension. Her doctors think she died of anguish and stress due to JJ's horrible demise.

In court we listened as FBI Special Agent Dr. Steve Daniels, Forensic Pathologist Dr. Garth Warren, and FBI Forensic Anthropologist Dr. Angi Christensen testified about JJ's autopsy and cause of death. It was "asphyxia by plastic bag and duct tape over the mouth."

Rexburg detectives and the FBI Evidence Response Team (ERT) searched the backyard and found a spot by a dry pond where the grass was lower than the surrounding grass. They carefully, methodically started digging.

We were shown pictures of each step, taken while police carefully exhumed JJ's body. The first things they found were stones placed flat and in an unnatural order. They removed the stones and found plywood under them. When they removed the plywood, according to Rexburg Detective Ray Hermosillo, they could smell the smell they all knew to be that of human remains. When they began to pull the dirt away, they could see black plastic like a garbage bag. They tore a small hole in the bag until they could see what looked to them like human hair sticking out of it.

On the witness stand, Detective Hermosillo described how they tore a small bit of the plastic away until they could see human hair. They painstakingly removed the dirt around JJ's body until they could pull away enough of the plastic to verify that it was indeed a human body.

In court, we were shown pictures of JJ's exhumed body still in the red pajamas. He had a white plastic bag over his head wrapped in duct tape. His legs and wrists were also wrapped with duct tape. Remember, according to Lori Daybell, binding was one of the ways to extract a zombie from someone's body.

I can't tell you the effect this and the pictures of Tylee's remains had on me, and I suspect my fellow jurors. Words like horrifying, terrible, and sad don't even begin to describe what I was feeling—and still do. Anger doesn't either. It was all of that and so much more. All of us, all 18 of us, were in shock and stunned. Many of us had lost control of our emotions and were openly crying in court. I knew this was going to be bad, but nothing prepared me for it. Nothing could have. No amount of warning me ahead of time and knowing we were going to see pictures of the remains prepared me for the facts we were confronted with. Everything I thought we knew about humanity and life changed at that moment. I was turned into something different than I had been. I don't know how else to describe it. I felt like I was confronted with a monster, and she was sitting there right in front of me. By this point in the trial, I don't think Lori Daybell had a chance. She was slumped as far down in her chair as she could be with her head turned as far as she could turn it to her right. She had nowhere to go, and she knew it.

JJ's blood was tested in Quantico and a small amount of GHB or Ecstasy was found. Apparently that could have been a component of the drugs he took to help with his autism, but I think it might also have been given to him just prior to his being murdered. I mentioned this idea while being interviewed on Hidden: A True Crime Podcast with Lauren and Dr. John, and Kay Woodcock messaged us that he was not drugged. I'm not sure how she knows this, but I don't think she would say it if it was not true.

Others in the courtroom were unable to control their emotions seeing what had been done to JJ. Lori Daybell refused to look at the pictures and appeared to be trying not to listen as the witnesses described what they found.

To differing degrees, everyone in that courtroom had become Lori Daybell's victims. Larry and Kay Woodcock will live it the rest of their lives and I can't see how they can ever live a "normal" life after this.

The detectives and agents who had to dig up the bodies are also her victims. They had to experience the horror firsthand. How can they possibly erase the images and smells from their minds? They can't. They were composed and professional on the witness stand in court, but I know what they must have been feeling inside. My heart goes out to them.

I think of the families. People with the names Vallow and Daybell. Now infamous names. I have gotten to know some of them personally and I know who they are. But I think about the kids in school with those names. Will they be treated differently? I think they must be to some extent. It's not fair, of course. They are good people just like you and me. They just happen to have had someone in their family who committed these atrocities. It shouldn't reflect on the rest of the families, but people being people, they will be curious at least.

The witnesses, some who thought they were Lori Daybell's friends but at some point found out they were simply her pawns, were players who to some degree took part in Lori Daybell's horrific acts. Sure, they were gullible, and we can even be angry at some of them for their stupidity and their part in this story, but I think some of these people will have a hard time living with what happened. Some may even have known what Lori Daybell was capable of, but I think most people have a conscience and will be remorseful of whatever their part was. They will have to live with themselves, and they know that, according to their religion, they will have to answer to God someday.

Even those of us in the courtroom who were not in any way associated with Tylee and JJ prior to the trial now see the world in a different light. Something has been taken away from us for the rest of our lives and we'll never get it back. Even as I write this book, I have to break away at times. Even so, it's useless. Whatever other activity I go and do, I still can't keep my mind off the many, many victims.

CHAPTER 17:
WAS SHE INSANE?

Insanity: *"The inability to see the world as it really is."*

There are a lot of meanings, but that's my definition of insanity. Nuts, isn't it? But how do you really define someone as insane? I think of the guy on the street ranting to someone I guess he imagines is there. Totally unaware of what's going on around him. If you've ever been to San Francisco or Portland, you've seen him.

But Lori Daybell isn't ranting and raving at some imaginary person. At least not outwardly. Still, she seems to believe some pretty weird stuff. Does she believe the things she says? Or is she so manipulative that she'll say anything to get people to go along with her? I wish I had the answer.

If you think she believes her kids were truly taken over by zombies, if you think she believes the only way to save their souls was to kill them in the brutal way they were killed, then I think you have to say she's insane. The alternative would be that you think she is right. Or at least you think she really believes these incredible things.

Some states will allow a plea of not guilty by reason of insanity. If a defendant is deemed to be insane, then they are not guilty of whatever crimes they committed. They are not considered capable of forming the intent to kill. However, it's not that they get off the hook completely. It usually means that instead of going to some prison like San Quinton or Pelican Bay, they go to an insane asylum, which I'm told isn't any better. The kicker is that once they are deemed to be rehabilitated, or sane, they are free. So it's not necessarily a life sentence.

Idaho doesn't allow insanity as a defense. Once you are deemed fit for trial, you go straight to trial, and if you are charged with something as serious as murder, you spend your time locked up in an asylum until you are deemed fit for trial. That's what happened with Lori Daybell. She spent 10 months being evaluated, and as soon as she was deemed fit for trial, Judge Boyce set the date.

I'm so thankful that Idaho has the sense to not let someone off just because they are deemed insane. I can't imagine the frustration it would cause if Lori Daybell were released because she was insane and then rehabilitated. The whole trial would have been different. It would have been focused on her sanity, the defense trying to prove she was insane, the prosecution trying to prove she knew what she had done. It would not have been fair to the victims, living or dead.

I will say that, having listened to Prosecutor Rachael Smith's questioning of Zulema Pastenes, it seems clear to me that Lori Daybell knew exactly what she was doing in her conversations with Zulema and that she was very strongly manipulating her.

Zulema seems to be a very manipulatable person to me. I don't mean to say that Zulema is dumb. In fact, she seems very intelligent, but she very much believed what Chad and Lori Daybell were telling her. I think Zulema just wanted to believe in a higher power and that Chad and Lori Daybell had a direct connection with that higher power. I think she was looking for answers. This points to the idea that Lori Daybell is not insane, just extremely manipulative and willing to take advantage of people.

Some of the people close to Lori Daybell say she changed after meeting Chad Daybell. In her testimony in court, Lori Vallow Daybell's former good friend, April Raymond, said Lori Vallow had been a good mother, a good wife to Charles, and a good friend prior to meeting Chad Daybell, but after meeting him, she changed. If it were true, if Lori Vallow had been just your normal Mormon housewife and mother before meeting Chad Daybell, then we would have to believe Chad Daybell was the kingpin and the evil manipulator, and Lori Vallow Daybell was his victim.

Nobody on the jury thought that. Twelve out of twelve jurors for sure, and I think eighteen out of eighteen jurors, after listening to all of the testimony, were ready to bang the (imaginary) gavel down and say she was guilty as hell. No excuses and nothing but pure disdain for her.

In fact, by the end of the trial, emotions were impossible to hide. Jurors were openly crying, and I could see the anger in their faces. No one had one ounce of sympathy for her. I truly believe nothing the defense could have come up with after so many days of listening to the witnesses for the prosecution could have changed that.

As an admittedly superficial sidenote, I was really disappointed that Judge Boyce didn't use a gavel. He was definitely not the judge you see in the movies. I'm not taking anything away from him. He was very effective, and I think respected by all. He just had a more quiet, calm way. Still, a few fireworks might have broken the tension.

Anyway, I don't believe the argument that Lori Daybell changed after meeting Chad Daybell. I also think she must have had something to do with the death of ex-husband Joe Ryan. Just too coincidental and we could plainly see what she was capable of. I simply think she and Chad Daybell were two people the world could have done without individually, but the two happening to come together was a travesty. They played off each other and used, manipulated, murdered, and threatened anyone in their path.

CHAPTER 18:
LORI AND CHAD'S LOVE AFFAIR

None of us would want the intimate details of our love lives shared with the world. Our little intimacies with our lovers are yucky to anyone else, and inappropriate for the world to hear.

I tried to be open minded while listening to FBI Special Agent Nathan Hart read the texts between Chad Daybell and Lori Vallow and listening to Zulema Pastenes describing what she saw and heard. However, given what we had already learned about the two and given the fact that they both were married to other people at the start of their relationship, I almost needed the barf bags that were handed to us earlier, listening to this particular testimony.

The texts between the two were read by Special Agent Hart and shown on the screen. I know the prosecution wanted him to read the texts out loud to get the full effect, but what must he have been thinking about having to read them? My guess is that he was thinking he would do whatever it takes to bring her down. He was extremely professional on the witness stand and did what it took to present the evidence he had found.

We listened to Special Agent Hart in Chapter 14 read some of the texts between Chad Daybell and Lori Vallow. Chad Daybell talked about "loin fire" and something about a storm in his pants. He talked about Lori Vallow wrapping her hands around the storm. I mean, come on, who talks like that?

The message I got was that Chad Daybell and Lori Vallow were two twisted people. They were incapable of being real, even with each other. They had to live in this crazy world of twisted scripture, half-truths, and justification of their actions. They had to make people in their inner circle believe they had been together many times on this earth to justify their illicit romance.

Lori Vallow had already declared that she received visions and messages from angels before ever meeting Chad Daybell, so to her it had to feel like it was meant to be when Chad Daybell told her on their first meeting that they had been married in a previous life. The devil himself couldn't have envisioned a more imperfect union. Two more manipulative, narcissistic people finding each other is hard to fathom, but as we've seen, it happens.

Lori Vallow was aware of Chad Daybell before they ever met. I think she sought him out after reading his books, listening to his podcasts, and hearing about him from friends in her church, so maybe it wasn't just a chance meeting.

According to Melanie Gibb's testimony, when Lori Vallow and Chad Daybell met at the *Preparing a People* conference in Utah in 2018, Lori Vallow immediately started flirting and spending as much time as she could at Chad Daybell's table.

On the stand Gibb said, "There was definitely an attraction from the very beginning. She seemed very interested in him. She seemed flattered by him, enticed by the conversation, a little flirty like." Gibb further testified that Lori Vallow already believed she'd had multiple lives before she met Chad Daybell.

Gibb also testified that Chad Daybell told Lori Vallow "they had been reunited again in their current life and had been sealed together for eternity by Jesus Christ." And they had been selected by Jesus to lead the 144,000 people who would remain on earth to do missionary work.

Gibb says Chad Daybell and Lori Vallow met several times at hotels while they were still married to other people, but Lori Vallow felt that their affair was okay. "She felt it was God's will," and they had been married together in previous lives and had a mission together. Gibb further testified that after Charles' death, "there was happiness and excitement between Chad and Lori."

At the *Preparing a People* Conference, Lori Vallow said she would sell every one of his books, and apparently she almost did, selling way more books than he would have been able to have done without her. She used her charms to ingratiate herself to him and it worked.

After meeting, it didn't take long for the courtship to continue. According to Gibb, both Chad Daybell and Lori Vallow were unsatisfied in their marriages, and both had previously said their spouses would pass away as both had been taken over by evil spirits.

In June, 2019, Lori Vallow sent an email to Chad Daybell claiming to be her husband Charles. In the email "Charles" invited Chad Daybell to Arizona to help Charles with a book he was supposedly writing, of course giving Chad Daybell an excuse to give to his wife Tammy to fly to Arizona to see Lori Vallow. Here is the text of that email:

> *Hello Chad,*
>
> *Hope you are doing well. This is Charles Vallow from Arizona. We really enjoyed having you stay with us in November when you came to the Preparing a People Conference. I appreciated you taking time to talk to me about the book I've been working on. Well, more than 6 months later I still haven't made much progress on it, but I feel an urgency to get it done.*
>
> *So I will cut to the chase. I'm willing to pay you well to help me get this book into shape as my ghostwriter. I really liked your autobiography and the tone you took in sharing experiences without preaching. Is there any way you could come here for*

a couple of days to help me get the book underway? I feel talking in person would be much more valuable than a phone call or video chat, mainly because I would like you to read through some of my journals and explain to me how the publishing industry works.

I'm out of town until Saturday but would gladly fly you down here early next week before the holiday and cover your expenses. You could stay in our guest room like before, or in a hotel if you prefer. I hate to take you away from your family, but I know this book is vital to my speaking success. I understand if you don't want to take part in the project, but I would definitely make it worth your time.

With Admiration,
Charles

Charles somehow found and read this email. It confirmed his suspicions, and he went on the offensive, still hoping to win Lori Vallow back. In fact, he sent a copy of the letter to Lori Vallow's brother Adam, hoping Adam would help him get through to her. Along with the letter, Charles sent this note to Adam:

Adam,

Open this letter and see what she did. I'm not sure of the relationship with her and Chad Daybell but they are up to something. She created an email alias for me as I've never set this one up. She sent this yesterday and I guess she forgot all her emails are on the computer at my house. I asked her to explain it and she started blaming you, Brandon and me for perpetuating a scheme against her. [Typical narcissistic behavior when caught.] Just more of her paranoia. She will not explain it. I am going to send it to Chad Daybell's wife. Her name is Tammy, and I found her email address on their website. I've got her cell number too. Sounds very suspicious to me. What do you think?

Whenever she gets caught doing this kind of stuff she starts blaming everybody else. Mostly me, you and Brandon. Brandon and I are victims of her craziness. I wish you luck trying to help her. I was the only one brave enough to try to get her help in January and look what happened to me. The whole family put a scarlet letter on me. Maybe now they can see what they're up against.

Thanks

Unfortunately for Charles he had just sealed his own fate. Lori Vallow and Chad Daybell couldn't let Charles tell Tammy about the affair. A few weeks later Alex shot Charles twice with a .45 caliber handgun. Charles was the first (that we are sure of) to be put out of the way of Lori Vallow and Chad Daybell's schemes.

Unfortunately for Lori Vallow, as we know, she would not be receiving the million-dollar prize for killing Charles. She would, however, receive almost $4,000 per month in Social Security payments meant for Tylee and JJ.

As it happened, Chad Daybell had had a speaking event in Arizona the prior November, 2018. Chad Daybell, Melanie Gibb, and a few others spent the night at Lori Vallow's house during that time. On the stand, Gibb describes a conversation Chad Daybell and Lori Vallow were having about sleeping arrangements. She said the conversation sounded contrived and she suspected the two would be sleeping together. Of course, husband Charles was out of town.

It was sometime after this that Chad Daybell convinced Lori Vallow to move to Rexburg. She needed to be there to help him prepare for the "end of days" or the "second coming of Christ." About a month and a half after Alex shot Charles, she did move to Rexburg along with brother Alex and niece Melani Boudreaux (now Pawlowski).

Raphael and Lili were two other names the couple called themselves, and Chad Daybell referred to Lori Vallow as his "goddess lover."

It seems to me that narcissism plays a role here. Chad Daybell was taken by Lori Vallow's good looks, her deep blue eyes, and long blond hair. He loved the attention she gave him and was totally taken in by her.

Lori Vallow, in turn, loved the attention she was getting from Chad Daybell. People wonder how someone with her good looks could be attracted to him, but I think she needed the attention. A better looking, more successful man might not dote over her and worship her like Chad Daybell did, and she craved this attention. Some of the videos we watched during the trial and some I have watched since show her manipulating or trying to manipulate people. She would use her good looks, her flirtatious manner, and her lilty voice to draw people in.

But it wasn't just a sexual attraction between the two. It went way deeper than that. It had to be for them to do the horrific things they did together. Their beliefs were uncannily similar. So much so that it can't be explained simply by their interests in the second coming of Christ or their religious beliefs.

Somewhere in my research I came across the term "folie a deux," and I have to admit, I had to look it up. It means "madness for two," and I think that describes Chad and Lori Daybell to a tee. They are both "mad," and more than that, they are both "mad" in the same way.

So, these two mad people who shared the same totally unfounded beliefs about religion found each other, and when they did, they became nuclear. A chain reaction like an atom bomb. They propped each other up and legitimized each other in their minds.

They were both thoroughly attracted to the idea that they were special, above everyone else in the eyes of God. Both claimed to be able to see behind the veil. Both claimed to have conversations with dead relatives and important people in the Bible. They were the chosen ones. In fact, they could not only choose who would survive the "end of days" and live on to lead the 144,000, but also, they got to decide who lived or died leading up to July, 2020.

PART 3:
AFTER THE TRIAL ENDED

CHAPTER 19:
THE VERDICT

After sitting through weeks of testimony, listening to at least 60 witnesses, after everything I have described to you, it was time for Judge Boyce to hand the case over to the jury. We had heard Rob Wood and Jim Archibald give us their closing arguments. After all of this, we heard the prosecution and defense rest.

There is no way for me to convey to you how much each of the 18 jurors had invested to this point. The fact was though, 6 of us had to go. Six of us would not get to be a part of deciding Lori Daybell's fate.

Of course we knew that was the deal. We were told how it would go down before the trial started, but that didn't make it any easier when my number was called, and I found out I would not be deliberating. Still, I was a free man now and I was excited about that.

Before we left the courthouse, Randy, the jury administrator, asked us if we would like to come back for the verdict. I immediately said I would. In fact, I wouldn't have missed it for anything. To be able to sit in the courtroom while the decision of 12 of my fellow jurors was read to Lori Daybell and the rest of the world was a thing I did not want to miss.

I asked if I could bring my wife, Susan, and Randy said he would make that happen. After all, even though we weren't able to talk about what happened in court, she had lived this with me. She followed the case every day and when I came home, even though we didn't talk about it, she knew what I had been through. It made me very thankful that I had her to come home to.

Still, people were lined up for hours every day hoping to get into the courtroom. They had to wait to see if they would win the lottery to get in, and of course, most of the people who wanted to get in did not. It was first come, first served for the verdict and I found out later from Nate Eaton that it also applied to the media. So getting a seat for the verdict was a big deal and it made us feel appreciated.

I got a kick out of listening to Susan describe her experience later when we were finally able to talk about it. She got to go for a drink with me and a few of the other jurors after the verdict and here's how I remember her describing it to us:

She rode in the van with us into the basement of the courthouse. We were closely guarded as we made our way up the elevator, down the long hall, and into the courtroom. Susan and I were separated at that point. My fellow alternate jurors and I were seated behind Lori Daybell. Our bailiff, Ken, marched Susan past all the other visitors to the front of the gallery and seated her next to the sketch artist, Lisa Cheney (who also provided the cover and most of the illustrations for this book). The courtroom was full and hushed with anticipation, wondering who Susan was, why she was there, and what made her important enough to be personally conducted to her seat by the bailiff. People asked her if she was family of the defendant. Susan just said no, she was just a citizen, I guess not really knowing what to say.

Susan was overwhelmed by the heaviness of it all. She was face to face with Lori Daybell for the first time, getting a real-life idea of what I had been through.

It was a huge relief to me when the verdict was read, and Lori Daybell was found guilty on all counts. Being behind her, I didn't get to see her face as the verdict was read, but people told me later that she just kind of scoffed and acted like it was not a big deal to her. It was a big deal to me. One of the jurors I talked to later, who could see her face, said, Lori Daybell had zero expression. She just stared off in one direction.

Court was quickly adjourned, and the courtroom was emptied out. I was escorted out the back by Ken and Steve. On our way out, Ken asked me where my wife was and I told him I didn't know, he was supposed to have taken charge of her. We moved down the hall as Ken went back to find her.

Susan described to me later that Ken conducted her down the same hall behind the courtroom I had just walked down. Lori Daybell was now there surrounded by guards, shackled into a wheelchair, blocking their way in the narrow hall. Susan and Ken had to squeeze by her. Her forced proximity to Daybell in that tiny hallway really gave Susan the creeps.

Anyway, the verdict was in, but my journey had just begun. I had determined by this point to write this book and I had a lot of work to do. There were several people who I needed to talk to and I had a million blanks to fill about the case.

CHAPTER 20:
THE DAYBELL PROPERTY AND
JJ AND TYLEE'S BURIAL SITES

July 30, 2023 was a typical clear blue Idaho summer day that Sunday as I drove 4½ hours east on Hwy. 84 and Hwy. 86 from Boise to St. Anthony, Idaho. The following morning would be Lori Daybell's sentencing and I wouldn't miss it.

St. Anthony is the Fremont County seat, and Fremont and Madison Counties are where the crimes were committed. Even though the trial had been moved to Boise, the sentencing would take place closer to home.

On the way to St. Anthony, I drove by Register Rock where you can still see the names of the Oregon Trail emigrants carved into the rock. Hwy. 84 and Hwy. 86 closely follow the Oregon Trail and there are several places to stop, read about, and see firsthand the history of the westward migration that took place mostly from the California gold rush in 1849 to May 10, 1869 when the golden spike was driven into the railbed in Promontory Summit, Utah Territory, tying the eastern and western ends of the cross-country railroad.

There are several places just a short drive from the highway where you can still see the ruts carved out by the mule or oxen driven wagons 170 years ago. It's in my DNA to drive or hike miles just to look at them.

My wife says, well, they're ruts, they look a lot like the last ruts we looked at. For me though, when I look at the ruts, I see the wagons and the people and beasts of burden and wonder at the hardship and sacrifice they made settling the West. What drove them? How could they have done it? I think for a lot of us living here in the West, the story intrigues us and inspires us. It actually kind of defines us in a way.

St. Anthony is home to the St. Anthony Sand Dunes and sits on the Henry's Fork River which is renowned for its blue-ribbon trout fishing. It's just a short drive from St. Anthony to West Yellowstone and the western entrance to Yellowstone National Park. It's a sparkling clean small city of under 4,000 inhabitants.

St. Anthony is also home to the Fremont County Courthouse where Lori Daybell's sentencing was to take place at 9am the following day. St. Anthony is 7% Catholic, 1.2% Lutheran, 0.8% Methodist, 0.3% Baptist, 0% Episcopalian, and most of the rest are Mormon, so it is overwhelmingly Mormon.

St. Anthony was founded in 1888 by members of the Church of Jesus Christ of Latter-Day Saints. The Yellowstone Tabernacle of the Church of Jesus Christ of Latter-Day Saints was erected there in 1912.

The Fremont County Courthouse was built in 1909 and is listed on the National Registry of Historic Buildings. In a time where old buildings were torn down long ago in the surge of population increase, this building truly is a monument to what Idaho stands for. When it was built, it was the most imposing building in the small city, and it still is. I like the fact that it remains standing and represents more of what justice used to be, and still should be, and for the most part at least, still is in places like St. Anthony, Idaho.

I think that because St. Anthony is 89% white, and because it's in Idaho, people make the assumption that it's racist, home of white supremacists. While to some very small extent that may be true, the historical reason that it's 89% white is that African Americans were originally sent to the plantations in the South and moved north to places like Baltimore and Chicago during the industrial revolution following the Civil War. Places like St. Anthony and Idaho, on the whole, are not places that had much to offer African Americans, or to anyone migrating out of the South after the Civil War. The farming and ranching, which was about all that was going on there at the time, were mostly done by the families that owned the farms and ranches.

Still though, while the Mormon Church did accept people of color since its inception, it did not allow people of color to move up in their ranks until 1978. African American members of the Mormon Church now say they are mostly happy with the church, but racism still exists among some of its members.

I have spent a lot of time in small-town Idaho, and I have heard the "n" word used more than once. Not like you hear it in rap music, but the old-fashioned way. It's pretty shocking to hear. I'm not excusing it in any way, but I do think it's easy for some people to say it in a place where no African American people are around to hear it.

I guess it comes with being in a place that hasn't changed much since before the Civil Rights movement of the '50s and '60s. It's one of the downsides, and that side is not pretty. I will say, however, that I think small-town Idaho gets a bad rap in that regard. My experience is that, on the whole, people are warm, welcoming, and honestly caring for whoever they cross paths with, no matter the color of their skin. The majority of people are genuinely kind and giving.

Back to the point of this chapter:

I couldn't go to St. Anthony without driving by the Daybell property. Not that I was drawn to see where JJ and Tylee had been so disrespectfully put into the ground, but for the sake of this book. Honestly, after looking at numerous pictures of the site in court, I felt I knew the property very well. I knew exactly where each of the children were buried.

Part of me would have liked to walk out to the two burial sites just to honor them, but I was told that Chad Daybell's adult kids still live in the house. I'm not sure if that is true, but the grass was green and in fact being watered, so out of respect for them and what they must still be going through, I left it alone. I did, however, linger on the street in my car thinking about them and what they must have gone through. I thought the property may have been abandoned, but since someone obviously still lives there, the yard is well kept and mowed.

According to an article by Clare Trapasso, Chad Daybell quitclaimed the house and property to his attorney John J. Prior. Idaho criminal defense lawyer Jeromy Stafford says, "No reputable lawyer would take a case with a quitclaim house, it's what low level, shady lawyers do."

According to Realtor.com, it is extremely hard to sell a house that is so infamous. Randal Bell of the Landmark Research Group in Laguna Beach, CA says, "It's a crime that involves kids, It's the worst kind of crime there is. It's in a rural area and rural areas tend to fare worse than suburban or urban areas when it comes to a crime scene.... They don't happen very often."

You can imagine that someone living in the house, even if they could get past the fact that three people were either murdered or buried there, would have to put up with being harassed by people interested in seeing where it all happened.

Still, it looks like every other property on the street. Most of the houses look to have been built around the middle of the 20th century and they all have at least an acre or two of land, some a lot more. I guess they were probably initially small farms or ranches. At least places where people could have a few horses, cows, and a big garden. The remnants of the monument to the kids people had placed along the fence were gone.

While I was parked there, I also thought of the people who still had hope, who still supported Chad Daybell, who put flowers and cards along the fence, hoping JJ and Tylee would be found alive. What must they have felt when they found out the bodies had been buried right behind that fence?

I know, in my mind's eye, as I sat alone in my truck, I could see the police searching the property on June 9, 2020, while Chad Daybell sat in his car in the driveway talking to Lori Daybell on the phone from her jail. The conversation had been recorded and we listened to it in court while Detective Hermosillo was on the stand. Chad Daybell sounded scared as he told Lori Daybell the police were searching the property.

According to Hermosillo's testimony, he could see Chad Daybell looking over his shoulder in the direction of JJ's gravesite. His assumption was that Chad Daybell was watching the police who were searching the area for evidence of a recent grave.

Chad Daybell drove off at a high rate of speed shortly after talking to Lori Daybell, and the police had to chase him down and arrest him. This happened right after the police discovered what they expected to be JJ, wrapped in plastic.

As I looked over the fence at the property and location of where Tylee and JJ were found, I recalled that this is when the jury was exposed to the first pictures of JJ's body. In the pictures we could see, partly exposed in the dirt, white plastic under black plastic, wrapped in duct tape, and what looked like human hair sticking out of a very small hole in the plastic that detectives said they had carefully cut open.

Shortly after this, what was left of Tylee's body was found in the family "pet cemetery." We listened for hours as Hermosillo described what that was like. As I sat in my pickup truck looking over the fence at the property and location of Tylee's temporary grave, the pictures of what was left of her came back to me vividly. The awning or whatever it was, and the dog statue were gone, but the firepit was still there and I could easily see where Tylee had been buried.

As I drove away in silence, I felt a heaviness and darkness that I had felt a few times before during the trial and I was a little sorry I had gone out there.

What happened next is kind of indicative of how this whole thing serving on this jury has gone for me and it's really why I am writing this book.

I checked into the hotel and found my two fellow jurors who were already there. When I made the reservation for this hotel, I had no idea that everyone I would want to connect with was staying at the same place. There are only a couple of hotels in Rexburg, but still, I felt extremely lucky to have picked the right one without even thinking about it. We talked and I told them I had been out to Chad Daybell's house. They were disappointed because they wanted to go out and were hoping I would go with them. I really didn't want to but said I would go with them because I didn't want to send them out there without me. I knew it would be emotional for them.

This time when we turned onto road 200N, the lonely turnout where I had parked just an hour or so earlier was now full of people. They had come from wherever they lived for the sentencing, and apparently the media was going wherever Kay and Larry were going. We parked, got out of the car, and approached. We could see that a memorial to Tylee, JJ, and Tammy had been put together on a neighbor's fence across from the Daybell property. I spotted Larry and Kay Woodcock right away. I had talked to them on the phone a few times and they knew I was writing a book. I was a little nervous to meet them in person, not knowing how they would react to me approaching them at that moment.

When we introduced ourselves, they instantly pulled us in and hugged us and thanked us for serving on the jury. I can still feel the warmth that came from them. These two people, who had suffered so much, turned everything around for me at that moment. They were comforting *me*. How cool was that! And that turned out to be the theme for the whole time I was there.

Just by coincidence, we were staying at the same hotel along with other of their family members, friends and of course a lot of media people who were also warm, welcoming and generous.

I spent a lot of time with Kay and Larry over the next two days, and I am happy to count them as friends. They answered all of my many questions and seemed to have no limit to their energy. Between being pulled this way and that way and being interviewed over and over again, they would sit there and talk. I had a list of questions for them that I don't think I ever got to. It was too interesting to just sit with them and chat about the trial, JJ, Tylee, Charles, and their lives with them.

CHAPTER 21:
SENTENCING

I was looking forward to finally wrapping up Lori Daybell's part in the case and seeing her get the life sentence I thought

Judge Boyce was sure to hand down. Life without the possibility of parole. That's what I was hoping for. She still was due to be extradited to Arizona for the murder of ex-husband Charles Vallow and, as I found out later, the attempted murder of her niece's ex-husband, Brandon Boudreaux. I think the trial in Arizona will happen after the Chad Daybell trial in Idaho, so nothing will be held back. I can't wait to see how that goes.

Since I was going to be in St. Anthony and since a lot of the principals in this case would also be there, I planned several interviews in preparation for writing this book.

I first talked to two of my fellow jurors. They had also studied this case since the trial ended, and we had a great conversation now that we were free to talk about it. I mentioned one of the two earlier in the book. She's the one of the two who I was most concerned about. I'm happy to say she is doing much better. The other says prayer has helped her through and she seems to be doing fine.

They did tell me that a younger woman who served with us is not doing as well. I think she was too young to be exposed to what she experienced in court. I don't think it was fair to her. Being as young as she was, she didn't have the life experience of someone older, who could hopefully process all this better, and I think it was too much of a shock to her. Also, she is the same age as Tylee would have been, and that would have to have had an effect on her. I know she has taken advantage of the counseling, paid for by the court, and I hope that helps her. She has been attending the Chad Daybell trial with me occasionally and I am getting to know her better. I'm finding out she is a very bright young lady with a great outlook on life. I think I somewhat unfairly place my hopes on her for her future, but I can't help wanting to see her succeed and have a happy life.

The sentencing was scheduled for 9am, Monday, July 31, 2023 at the Fremont County Courthouse in St. Anthony, Idaho.

When I got there, there was already a big crowd hoping to get into the courthouse. Media was everywhere. This time I would not be secreted into the basement of the courthouse and isolated from the media. I was not, however, allowed to walk in the front door like everyone else. The four of us jurors who came to see the sentencing were led to the west side of the courthouse and escorted inside.

Security was everywhere. No one was allowed into the courtroom without going through security. Everyone had to show their ID and tell why they were there. I'm sure they were prepared for anything that might happen; somebody angry enough at Lori Daybell to attempt to get to her in court, someone trying to free her, or just some nut job trying to make a name for himself. Who knows, but whatever it might be, they were ready for it. Fortunately, but not surprisingly, things went perfectly smoothly.

The inside of the courthouse is the same as it was over 100 years ago. It made me wonder what cases have been tried there over the years. If you've ever watched the movie *True Grit*, with John Wayne as Rooster Cogburn and Kim Darby as Mattie Ross, this courthouse looked a lot like the one in Fort Smith, wood floors and all. Super cool. I also thought Judge Boyce looked like he felt more at home here.

I couldn't help but notice the twelve seats for the jury must have also been built in 1908. They were very cool, built of wood and cast iron. Sturdy as could be, but they didn't look very comfortable. I could imagine past juries sitting in those chairs waving the little fans people used to use to cool off.

By 9am everyone was in their seats watching quietly as Lori Daybell entered the courtroom, her shackles clattering on the wood floor as she hobbled in, escorted by two deputies. During the trial she was allowed to dress nicely and fix herself up, but not this time. She was wearing orange and white striped coveralls. She was in handcuffs and her ankles were shackled.

Before Judge Boyce handed down his sentence, four people were allowed to give impact statements. I thought it would have been better if they were facing Lori Daybell, but she was on the left, sitting between her attorneys, Mr. Archibald and Mr. Thomas, facing the judge, and the people speaking were on the right, also facing the judge.

We first heard from Tammy Daybell's sister, Samantha Gwilliam. As Samantha spoke, it looked to me like Lori Daybell was doing her best to look away, holding her head down.

Samantha talked about how Lori Daybell had to pay for her actions according to the laws of man and would still answer to the laws of God after passing from this life. She said she had researched Lori Daybell after she met Chad and found nothing but lies.

Speaking directly to Lori Daybell she said, "You are not exalted beings, and your behavior makes you ineligible to be one." She went on to say, "You could have easily divorced your spouses and made your own perverted lives together, but you needed money. You are a liar, an adulteress and a murderer. Your trial was the last thing my mother had to live through. She declined in health as she heard through news reports all the terrible things that happened, and she had to relive all the things we have tried to forget the last four years. My mother passed away in June knowing that you will never come out of prison again."

After the sentencing I had the opportunity to visit with Tammy Daybell's aunt, Vicki Hoban, who said Lori Daybell's reaction was shameful as Samantha spoke. She was right. Lori Daybell actually giggled at times.

In her impact statement, Vicki said, "Instead of getting a good night's sleep, she [Tammy] was brutally executed in her own bed. She was taken from us by murdering thieves. Tammy was robbed of her entire life and her family of ever seeing her again. You [Lori] are now going to pay the price, albeit never sufficient in this life, it's all we can do. I hope that the life you live is filled with fear and that every day you are terrified; the way beautiful Tylee lived in fear for hers and sweet JJ, as you continued terrifying her saying they would be zombies." She went on to say that her granddaughter and Tylee's group of friends were "stuck in their grief and sadness." Again, more victims for Lori Daybell.

I think the main point of Kay Woodcock's statement was that Lori Daybell was driven by greed and the need to be the center of attention. Woodcock also said, "I now realize what a nothing Chad Daybell is. A man with no ability to support anyone, no success of his own, a user of the weak minded, a lazy, good for nothing, spineless man that rode his wife's coattails of success."

The hardest part to listen to was when Kay described JJ's premature birth and his short life. She said she and Larry raised JJ themselves until he was 9 months old at which time Charles and Lori Vallow adopted him.

I don't think she said this during her statement, but I remember her telling of how JJ would lay quietly on Larry's chest. This was special because it would magically calm JJ down when nothing else worked. Being a grandfather myself and having been a grandson, I can say for sure that there is something very special about the bond between grandparents and grandkids.

What happened next was a shock to everyone in the courtroom. Judge Boyce gave Lori Daybell the opportunity to speak before he handed down his sentence and she actually had something to say. He called it the right of allocution.

Allocution is defined as the direct address between the judge and the convicted defendant prior to sentencing. We had not heard a word from Lori Daybell up to this moment. She made it clear through the looks on her face that she had so little respect for the proceedings it was beneath her to bother reacting in any way to what was being said about her in court.

What she had to say was so bizarre. It did, however to me at least, put an exclamation point on the whole trial.

Daybell read from something she must have prepared earlier. She starts by quoting Jesus in the New Testament of the Bible. "In John chapter 8, verse 7 Jesus says, 'He that is without sin among you, let him cast the first stone.'"

I have no idea what reaction she was looking for, but I can tell you that, for me, it was extremely insulting. She was comparing herself to all of us. To insinuate that we are all as bad as her is ridiculous.

She went on to say, "Jesus knows me, and Jesus understands me. I mourn with all of you who mourn for my children, and Tammy. Jesus Christ knows the truth of what happened here."

It gets more bizarre as she continued, "Jesus Christ knows that no one was murdered in this case. Accidental deaths happen, suicides happen. Fatal side effects from medication happen." My thought at the time was: Do people accidentally get buried in your husband's backyard?

She claims to have died on the hospital bed while birthing Tylee. That never happened. It had happened to a friend of hers who had told her the story. She claims that because of her near-death experience, she has access to heaven and the spirit world.

She said, "Since then, I have had many communications with people now living in heaven, including my children, Tylee Ashley and Joshua Jackson."

As she was speaking, I could see prosecuting attorney Lindsey Blake looking to her left at Lori Daybell in disbelief as Lori Daybell's own attorneys sat there stone-faced. What else could they do?

She went on to say that she talked directly to Jesus and Angels.

"Because of these communications I know for a fact that my children are happy and busy in the spirit world. Because of my communication with *my friend*, Tammy Daybell, I know that she is also very happy and extremely busy."

How could she possibly call Tammy her friend? She had nothing to do with Tammy prior to having an affair with Tammy's husband and murdering her.

"I know how wonderful heaven is and I'm homesick for it every day. I do not fear death, but I look forward to it."

A good argument against the death penalty. We would have been giving her what she wanted.

She said that after her near death experience, she was told to go back to earth by Jesus to complete things she was told to do. I guess she is trying to tell us Jesus told her to kill her own children, as well as Tammy and her husband Charles.

Lindsey Blake was visibly disgusted as Lori Daybell described how, after her supposed near death experience, she was asked by Jesus and agreed to go back to Earth to help her children and others.

"Tylee has visited me. She is happy and very busy. Tylee is free now from all the pain of her life. Tylee suffered horrible physical pain her whole life. I sat with her year after year after year, while she screamed in pain when the morphine wasn't even enough to take away the pain of her pancreatitis… and I'm the only person on this earth who knows how much Tylee suffered in her life."

Lori Daybell appeared to tear up as she was saying these things. I could tell it was totally contrived, and I guess she was expecting sympathy for all she had been through. If there was one person in that courtroom who felt anything like sympathy for her, I would love to talk to that person and ask how. How could anyone possibly feel anything but absolute disgust for her and what she did? And now she was rubbing it in our faces, apparently insisting that we excuse her for it.

In reference to Tylee, Lori Daybell added, "My whole life I tried to protect her." According to Lori Daybell, Tylee told her,

"Stop worrying mom, we are fine." And JJ told her, "you didn't do anything wrong mom."

Regarding Tammy, Lori Daybell said, "My eternal friend, Tammy Daybell has visited me, she came to bring me peace and comfort."

She ended by saying, "I look forward to the day we're all reunited, and I too will rest with them in the arms of my Jesus."

When she was finally done, it was time for Judge Boyce to hand down his sentence. I have to say that in the first half of his statement, he was making me and I'm sure everyone else in the courtroom a little nervous. It actually sounded like he was going to go light on her.

However, he ended with this: "It's unbelievable you have no criminal history, and yet, sit here convicted of the most serious criminal charges. The most unimaginable type of murder is having a mother murder her own children, and that's exactly what you did. Despite the jury convicting you, you still sit here before the court today and say you didn't do it… and brought them here to murder them when any other person would have gladly taken them. I don't think you have any remorse. When you knew the children were dead… they were found burned, mutilated… like animals."

He went on to say that he was traumatized by the photos of the dead victims and couldn't imagine how law enforcement felt who had to see it in person.

He added, "I don't believe a god in any religion would want what happened here to happen."

With that, it was finally time for Judge Boyce to hand down Lori Daybell's sentence. Everyone was on pins and needles waiting to hear what it would be and quite a few people were still wiping away tears, presumably of frustration after listening to Lori Daybell.

Lori Daybell sat there stone-faced as we all listened as Judge Boyce threw the book at her: Three consecutive life sentences and two concurrent life sentences plus a few years for the theft charge related to the social security death benefits that were meant for Tylee and JJ. She will never again see the light of day.

It's important that the life sentences are consecutive instead of concurrent. What it means is that even if she were somehow to be relieved of one of the sentences, the next one would start where that one left off. In other words, there is no chance of parole or getting out early for any reason until she is carried out in a body bag.

She will serve out her sentence at the Pocatello Women's Correctional Center in Pocatello, Idaho, except for when she is extradited to Arizona for her next trial. I have heard that even if she is convicted in Arizona, she will serve out her time in Pocatello.

As soon as the sentencing was over and court was adjourned, my fellow jurors and I were invited into Judge Boyce's chambers to finally talk to him. We had been isolated from him during the whole trial and were surprised and excited and honored by his invitation. With him in his chambers were his wife and his clerk. His clerk, Courtney, had sent the jurors a sketch, done by a sketch artist, of the jurors sitting in court, and it was good to have the opportunity to thank her for that in person. I felt it was very thoughtful of her.

I think a judge would have to be very good at hiding his emotions. He definitely showed no emotion in court. He seemed to tear up as he thanked us for our service as jurors. Seeing that, I could only imagine what it must have been like for him presiding over this trial. It must have been a huge relief for him to have it be finally over. He had been scrutinized and criticized by some in the media. He had to make sure that nothing went wrong that could jeopardize this case. He had to constantly consider the arguments of the attorneys on both sides and make fair decisions. I hope he is proud of himself for the way it all went. I am proud of him. He is slated to be the presiding judge in the Chad Daybell trial so he has a lot more work ahead of him on this case.

One of the things he did for the sake of the jury was to end court every day at 3:30. He said at the beginning of the trial that he would do that since it would be such a long trial and he wanted to make sure we had time to do the things required of life. He stuck to this promise throughout the trial, and it helped a lot.

After spending a half hour or so with Judge Boyce, we walked out of the courthouse. It was a hot day, and the sun was intense. Media was still everywhere, but they all seemed to be busy messing with their equipment. I guess they had just finished interviewing the people who they had wanted to interview as they walked out. Everyone else was gone.

That ended my experience as a juror on the Lori Daybell Vallow trial. I was left with nothing but my own thoughts. My initial thought was that it would take me years to sort out my feelings. I think writing this book has helped. My next thought was of all the people I had met and how they would do.

CHAPTER 22:
THE POKEY

It stands to reason that a nickname for the Pocatello Women's Correctional Center would be "the Pokey," but it doesn't derive its meaning from there. "Pokey" is slang for jail, but it actually comes from a 20th century British word "pogey," used to describe a poorhouse or "welfare hotel."

The Pocatello Women's Correctional Center (PWCC) was opened in April 1994, and houses 331 women inmates. There is one death row inmate at this time. Her name is Robin Row and, interestingly, she is convicted of killing her husband and two children for financial gain. Sound familiar? She is 65 years old and has been on death row for 30 years. I guess a death sentence doesn't necessarily mean you will be put to death, not very quickly at least.

I applied to the prison for a visit with Lori Daybell, inmate number 153745, in the one in a million chance that it would be granted by her. Interviewing her is not something I wanted to do, not on any level, other than that I am writing a book that is, to some small degree, about her. Of course, I was not granted that interview. Whew, dodged that bullet! I would have to be satisfied with learning what I could about the PWCC on the internet and by doing a drive-by, getting as close as I could without causing alarm.

The PWCC sits on a hill south of Pocatello overlooking the town and the Idaho State University. The warden, Janell Clement, describes it as a place of opportunity. A chance for the female inmates there to get their lives back in control by taking advantage of counseling and educational opportunities. I'm sure for some it is just that, but I doubt it will be anything like that for Lori Daybell.

From what I could see from the outside, it actually looks pretty nice as far as prisons go. The grounds are well kept and green. The buildings are made of colorful concrete blocks. The few windows I could see were narrow, too narrow for someone to get through. There is a lot of razor wire. No guard towers or armed guards were visible.

The women are housed in small cells with 7 other inmates. It is hard to move around when everyone is in the cell. There is one toilet per cell, and it is right out in the open. There is zero privacy and it's hard to imagine one would feel very safe. It usually takes two to four weeks for new inmates to be processed and injected into the general population. The inmates have to go through psychiatric evaluation during this process and I don't know if Lori Daybell will be held in a solitary cell for her own protection or if that is even an option.

The prison has a commissary where inmates can buy items to make their lives more livable if they have money in their accounts. A small bag of Cheetos is $9.00. Inmates can buy laptops, earphones, TVs, makeup, etc. The laptops are extremely limited as to what they are able to be used for.

People on the outside can send inmates money which can be spent in the commissary. In Lori Daybell's case, 20% of that money would be dedicated to paying her fines. Why it's not more, I don't know. Why would anyone send her money in the first place? I have heard that it is common for infamous inmates, such as her, to have a following. Hard to imagine, but it's true. She will likely receive money from someone on the outside which she will spend in the commissary. I think makeup will be what she spends it on.

Apparently she was pretty popular when she was in the county jail in Boise waiting for her trial. She had made friends and somehow brought fellow inmates into the fold. I don't know if she was able to convert any of them to her beliefs, but they even helped her prepare for a court appearance by making eye liner out of pencil lead and lipstick out of Jolly Ranchers. I didn't know this at the time of the trial, but I could see there was something off about the makeup she wore.

I don't know if that will happen for her at PWCC. I would imagine that the inmates there will be more "hardened" and possibly less gullible. I have heard that kid killers aren't exactly safe in prison, and I have to think that word will get around about who she is. I'm sure the inmates at PWCC were aware of her before she ever got there. Apparently true crime shows are popular entertainment for the inmates.

Here is an account, some of which was taken from an inmate who corresponds with Gigi on her Pretty Lies and Alibis Podcast, of how it goes when someone enters a women's correctional center: Inmates are asked who is to be called if they die, they are washed with disinfectant, they are strip searched along with whatever other inmates are entering with them. They are isolated for two weeks while they go through a psychiatric evaluation. During this isolation, even though they are alone in their cell, other inmates are sizing them up and they feel like they are on display. I don't know if Lori Daybell will be held in a solitary cell for her own protection or if that is even an option. I do know that Lori Daybell will be in maximum security and there are no open windows there.

When they are released into the general population, other inmates can be vicious, the food is sub-standard and it is overcrowded. All inmates see themselves as innocent victims and they tend to run in packs or gangs. It's primitive, the bunks are hard, and snitching gets you cut. Sure doesn't sound like a place anyone would want to be for any amount of time.

Prison is scary, humiliating, and humbling. The smells they are constantly subjected to are terrible. It's loud and some inmates use wet toilet paper in their ears to try to block out the noise. There are severely mentally ill inmates among the general population. Suicide and self-harm is common among new inmates. Guards have pet peeves, and you better learn them quickly. Lockdowns are common.

Higher profile inmates are targeted, and one would think especially inmates who hurt kids. They are always looking over their shoulder. We know that Lori Daybell was able to win over her fellow inmates while in the local jail in Boise, but it will be very different for her at the PWCC. Jail doesn't prepare you for state prison.

Inmates get three meals a day during the week and two on weekends. The food is substandard, yet somehow weight gain is still a problem. Clothes are washed twice a week and bedding once a week.

Apparently inmates being inmates, they have found a way of making hooch in the toilet. Tampons are used as curlers, although I'm not sure who would be concerned about their hair. Knowing what I know about Lori Daybell, she might be.

There is a Mormon Church right below the prison to the northeast. I couldn't see it from the parking lot because of the slope of the hill, and I don't think anyone would be able to see it from the prison. What can be seen are several steeples on Mormon Churches off in the distance. I don't know if Lori Daybell has a window, and if she does, which direction she can see, but I do think her religion is all she has left. I wonder if she looks out wishing she were free.

John Thomas, Lori Daybell's defense attorney, talked a lot about hope in his statement before Judge Boyce handed down his sentence. I really can't see any reason for her to be hopeful now.

She certainly has no hope of ever getting out of prison. She is human, however, and I guess it's in our nature to find some reason to be hopeful. Hopeful to get through the day maybe. Hopeful for redemption?

CHAPTER 23:
APPEALS

With such a stiff sentence and nothing to lose, of course Lori Daybell's attorneys would appeal the verdict. They appealed to examine the case, guilty verdict, and the sentence.

In fact I just read the appeal submitted by Lori Daybell's attorney, Jim Archibald. Among other things, it basically says that Lori Daybell was not mentally fit for trial and that Judge Boyce erred allowing her to be tried. The defense appealed based on 16 different issues in total. It also states that the prosecution's opening statement to the jury was unfair.

I have listened to the recording of Lindsey Blake's opening statement looking for what might be unfair in it, and I can't see what it could be. Especially since they proved everything they accused her of in the opening statement.

The appeal also contends that Lori Daybell was not afforded her right to a speedy trial. She had served 1200 days (about 3¼ years) in jail prior to her trial and that is not what I would consider speedy. There were several continuances granted by Judge Boyce to the prosecution.

I do have to say they might have somewhat of an argument here. However, the trial was held up for 10 months of that time due to Lori Daybell being evaluated for competency, so that also contributed to the delay. As we've seen, it was not your run of the mill murder case either. Also remember, everything was put in limbo by Covid 19 and the associated shutdowns.

I have had several friends contact me worried about the appeal, but as I tell them, she is allowed appeals. I think the chances of this case being overturned are very small. The defense is given 42 days by law to submit an appeal, so they had to get it done right away or lose their right to do it. Even if the trial were overturned and depending on the basis for overturning it, it would likely be remanded for a new trial. She wouldn't just be set free. I would hate to see a new trial happen. Putting more people through it all and some of the people through it again would be a travesty, but like I said, the chances of it being overturned are very small.

Lori Daybell had been in a mental institution for nearly a year before Judge Boyce determined she was fit to be tried. I have to wonder if her allocution statement at the sentencing was just a ploy to show she is insane. But remember, insanity is not a defense in Idaho. A defendant does, however, have to be deemed sane enough to understand what is happening at his or her trial and have the mental capacity to take part in his or her defense.

All I can say is that it would be infuriating at this point to have her trial voided because it was determined after the fact that she was not fit for trial.

I just think that there is a window for submitting an appeal, and of course they are going to submit one. But I doubt it will go anywhere. I also can't imagine her ever seeing the outside of prison.

Her appeal was submitted to the Idaho Supreme Court, and that court does not have to grant a hearing on her appeal. If they do decide to hear it, the Supreme Court justices are different judges, so it wouldn't be Judge Boyce. In the unlikely event that the Supreme Court overturned the trial, it would go back to the trial court, and it could be retried by a different judge, or possibly it could be Judge Boyce again.

CHAPTER 24:
EXTRADITED TO ARIZONA

As soon as the Idaho verdict was in, the state of Arizona Governor Katie Hobbs immediately filed the extradition papers to extradite Lori Daybell to Arizona. She is accused of murdering her husband Charles Vallow in order to receive the million-dollar payout on his life insurance and attempting to murder Brandon Boudreaux. Once the paperwork is filed, it takes 90 to 120 days to actually extradite her. Idaho Governor Brad Little has signed the extradition papers, allowing her to be sent to Arizona, but I don't know when she will go. I guess it will now be up to Arizona to set a court date.

It looks like they may have to wait for Lori Daybell's appeal to either be denied or heard by the Idaho Supreme Court, but I can't get a positive answer about that. *(Note: On November 30, 2023, just after midnight, Lori Daybell was extradited to Arizona and booked into Maricopa County Jail. Her trial is set for August 2024.)*

The evidence against her in Arizona looks pretty damning to me. Gilbert, AZ Detective David Duncan already testified in the Idaho Lori Daybell trial. He quoted Lori Daybell after Charles' murder: "I just got a letter from the insurance company, and I am not the beneficiary. It's a spear through my heart."

There is plenty of other evidence that will be submitted in the Arizona court: the bullet or bullet mark in the floor under Charles' dead body, Lori Daybell and Alex's lies, and conflicting statements told to police there, and other statements about Charles including saying that he was dark. I would think the most damning evidence will be what she has been convicted of in Idaho. They might not be able to use what happened in court in Idaho against her in court in Arizona, although felony convictions are sometimes admissible. The judge in Arizona will have to decide whether to exclude it or not.

Brandon Boudreaux also testified about what happened in Arizona. He talked about how he saw a rifle fitted with a silencer pointed out of the back window of what was later proven to be Tylee's Jeep as he was pulling into his driveway. The rifle went off and his driver's side window shattered right before he sped off and called 911.

There is plenty of evidence for that one, too. It was definitely Tylee's Jeep, but Tylee wasn't driving because she had been murdered. The rifle and suppressor were recovered in Lori Daybell's apartment in Idaho.

I also have to wonder if police in Arizona or maybe the FBI are looking into Lori Vallow's third husband, Joe Ryan's, death. He was said to have died of natural causes in his apartment in Phoenix on April 3, 2018. I just wonder if they are second guessing their determination after everything that has unfolded since. Especially since we know brother Alex tasered him and was convicted of it. They did revisit the possibility that Lori Ryan murdered him after she was accused in Idaho but they determined at that time that the original cause of death, a heart attack, was accurate.

Phoenix police do have a recording of Lori Ryan talking to a family member saying, "I was going to murder him, I was going to kill him like the scriptures say." Could this have been the first of Lori Ryan and brother Alex's murders, or was it a huge coincidence? Or maybe it wasn't even the first. Who knows at this point. It would be interesting to know. It would prove that she was already a murderer before meeting Chad Daybell, and I think she was, or at least was capable of it.

CHAPTER 25:
CHAD DAYBELL'S TRIAL

Boise's next big event in this sad saga is the Chad Daybell trial. It started on April 1, 2024, and is taking place at the same courthouse, with mostly the same prosecution team, and the same judge. Only the defense will be different. Chad Daybell has his own attorney, John Prior. I am putting myself through long days of sitting in court. Cameras are not allowed, but the court is livestreaming their own feed, so even if I miss a day, I will still be able to watch it and I will be in close contact with the media people who are there every day. I guess it's FOMO (fear of missing out) that keeps me there every day. I will say that, so far as of this writing, something important has happened every day I have been there. Someone different, related to the case, shows up, and I am able to gather new information. Or I might miss something that was said, and I can talk to Nate Eaton or Lauren Matthias, both of whom never miss a thing.

Judge Boyce has held regular hearings leading up to the trial. Chad Daybell's attorney, John Prior, is definitely putting up a fight. He has attacked prosecutor Rob Wood, saying he said things in the Lori Daybell trial that will affect the Chad Daybell trial. Rob Wood countered that Mr. Prior has taken his words out of context. Mr. Prior also criticized EastIdahoNews reporter Nate Eaton, claiming things he reported will affect the trial. The prosecution tried to get the trial moved to Rexburg, but Judge Boyce didn't allow it.

Chad Daybell is charged with three counts of murder and three counts of conspiracy to commit murder, for the deaths of his wife, Tammy, and Lori Daybell's children, Tylee and JJ.

I will save saying anything more about it until it is over, since I am writing another, more in-depth, book about Chad Daybell's trial, including what led up to it and what we might do to keep our children safe. I can't wait to hear what new evidence the prosecution has in store, and I wonder if Lori Daybell will testify. According to Section 9-203 of Idaho Code, she doesn't have to testify against her husband, and I can't think of anything she has to gain at this point other than maybe trying to clear her name by blaming it all on Chad Daybell. It does appear that Mr. Prior plans to go after everyone, including Lori Daybell.

I do think a lot of new information will come out. Some already has, and I'm hoping a lot more of my questions will be answered. More layers will be peeled back, exposing, I'm sure, ever more layers. With all the interest this case has instilled in people, in the prepper community, religious counselors, and the Mormon Church, I think there will have to be some kind of reckoning.

I wish the prosecution team luck and I hope they can all breathe a sigh of relief when it's over. I think it's extremely rare to have to try a case as horrific as Chad and Lori Daybell's. I know it has taken a toll on all of them as well as many other people, and my wish for them is to be able to get back to life as normal as possible. I hope they can focus on all the good people involved in these cases, as I have done, and take heart in that.

CHAPTER 26:
EPILOGUE

I took a lot away from my experience as a juror in this trial. I think some about the perpetrators, but mostly I think about the victims. I have a lot of hope for those who survived, and my hope is that they are able to move on with life in a positive way. I see strength in some of them that I would not have expected, so I am optimistic.

I have a renewed pride in my state and the legal system within it. I have a lot of pride and sincere admiration for the people who work in the legal system here.

I think the state of Arizona let everyone down to some extent as events unfolded early on in this case, but I can't conclude, in my own mind, after learning as much as I can about how things went down, that anyone is exactly at fault there. Before the kids were missing, there wasn't any reason not to believe Lori Vallow other than her and Alex's conflicting stories and the fact that Alex's second shot was made while Charles was on the floor.

I also think the police there had their hands tied to some extent when it came to helping Charles. It's easy to look back and say they should have done this, or they should have done that. Once they had direct evidence that a crime had been committed (the attempted shooting of Brandon), they were all over it, doing everything possible to solve the crime and protect Brandon. I'm pretty confident that justice will get served in Arizona when they finally get Lori Daybell in court.

I've talked a lot about the Mormon Church. We could say the Mormon Church let everyone down. I think maybe the institution of the Mormon Church did so to some degree, only because of its past and because the institution puts men on a pedestal, and putting men on a pedestal might have led to people believing Chad Daybell early on over some people like his sister-in-law, Heather Daybell, who knew who he really was. The Mormon Church is as American as any institution could possibly be. Its history is our history. I am not Mormon, and I hope I have treated the Mormon Church and its members fairly in this story.

It is interesting to me that Lori Daybell has not been excommunicated from the church. Or maybe she has been, but the church is keeping it quiet. Nobody seems to know for sure, but someone told me she probably has been, but perhaps the church just doesn't want to talk about it or announce it because they don't want to bring attention to their member or ex-member Lori Daybell. I don't understand that though. When Chad Daybell was excommunicated, it was all over the news.

Anyway, we are all imperfect and I think in the case of Arizona and in the case of the Mormon Church, we are doing our best. It was just an impossible situation and who would ever have believed what Chad and Lori Daybell were capable of?

After sitting through the hours and hours of testimony and looking at all the evidence provided by the state prosecutors, some of it horrific, I thought about the fact that Lori Daybell was not facing the death penalty. The most I could hope for was life in prison. Life in prison did not seem like enough justice to satisfy me.

After pondering that for some time, I realized that maybe life in prison *would* be more than what she deserved. She hadn't shown any remorse whatsoever to this point.

My hope is that at some point she will come to terms with what she has done. Maybe she will realize how many people she hurt. Maybe she will think of her many victims and feel remorse. Maybe she will re-read the Bible and think about how she twisted the scripture to suit her selfish wants. Maybe she will ask her Lord and Savior for forgiveness. That would be all the justice we can hope for.

We can't bring Tylee, JJ, Tammy, or Charles back. We can't punish people like Alex who are already dead. We can only hope to learn from experience and do what we can to keep such a horrific tragedy from happening again. We can support what is good in our world and deal with what is bad in whatever way is appropriate. We can learn from history, so we don't repeat our mistakes.

I plan to follow this book up with a sequel after the Chad Daybell trial. I'm confident there will be a lot more to write about. Until then...

CHAPTER 27:
SECOND EPILOGUE

One of the problems with writing a book about something so current, something that is actually still happening, is that new facts arise, and new developments happen. While I'm going to save a lot of what is upcoming for a future book, a sequel to this one after the Chad Daybell trial (that is of course, if this one is successful), I feel like there is one event that needs to be added here: JJ's celebration of life. It's not only a matter of closure for my book, but so much closure for the family and others who were close to JJ. Of course I didn't know JJ when he was alive, but in a way I do know him now, so I guess it's closure for me in a way too. His remains were finally released by Judge Boyce to the family on October 16, 2023, almost 4 years after his body was found buried in Chad Daybell's backyard. Unfortunately Tylee's remains continue to be held. I'm not sure why that is, but, hopefully, she too will be released and finally laid to rest. *(Note: Tylee's remains have also been released to the family since I finished my writing.)*

I do not know if JJ's celebration of life will be open to the public or when it will be, but I am hoping to attend. The same goes for Tylee's funeral, whenever that happens.

Appendix

In case you want to dive deeper into this case or keep up on new developments, I am including these resources:

My website: **http://tomevansauthor.com** (I'm not a blogger and I won't be giving regular updates, but I will announce some new information leading up to the Chad Daybell trial.)

Here are 3 podcasts that will keep you updated regularly:

Hidden: A True Crime Podcast: Dr. John and Lauren Matthais' podcast

Pretty Lies and Alibis: GiGi McKelvey's podcast

Silver Linings Podcast: Lori Daybell's uncle Rex and brother Adam

Here is a private Facebook group: *DOOMSDAY-Justice For J.J. & Tylee* (there are other Facebook pages dedicated to this case)

Here are 2 news outlets:

Nate Eaton: eastidahonews.com

Justin Lum with Fox 10 News in Phoenix

Here is the organization that I am donating profits of this book to:

Hope House Inc. **https://ahome2come2.com**

Hope House is an amazing nonprofit organization right here in Idaho that takes in kids in need from all over the world and gives them a home, love, education, and everything they need to succeed in life. Please take a minute to check them out. They make good use of any money you might want to donate in addition to what I send them from your purchase of this book.

About the Author

On April 1, 2023, I found myself in the jury box listening to opening arguments in the Lori Vallow Daybell trial. I did not want to be there and found the whole situation dark and depressing.

By the time the trial was over, I had a different point of view. In fact, I was proud of what I was seeing and honored to do my part.

I grew up in Northern California back in the '60s and '70s and spent most of my time in logging country fishing the Eel River, surf fishing in the ocean and riding dirt bikes through miles and miles of wilderness.

I spent the first five years of my adult life working in a sawmill as a millwright before heading to the city for college where I studied Architectural Engineering. In 1984 I was married while continuing my studies. I had to quit college when our first child was born and started designing and building custom homes.

In 2005 I moved myself, my wife and our two children to Idaho and continued my business. Shortly after that our foster daughter came into our lives full time.

My wife and I now have three adult children and three grandchildren.

By the time the trial was over, I knew two things, I was proud of what I saw and I wanted to find some way to have something good come out of it. I decided I would write about it and tell a story of all the good that I saw. And, I would donate proceeds of the book to an organization that helps children in need.

My book, *Money, Power and Sex, the Lori Vallow Daybell Trial by Juror Number 18*, is my humble attempt to tell my story.